sun signs

for writers

sun signs
for writers

BEV WALTON-PORTER

WRITER'S DIGEST BOOKS
Cincinnati, Ohio
www.writersdigest.com

SUN SIGNS FOR WRITERS. Copyright © 2006 by Bev Walton-Porter. Manufactured in China. All rights reserved. No other part of this book may be reproduced in any form or by any electronic or mechanical means including information storage and retrieval systems without permission in writing from the publisher, except by a reviewer, who may quote brief passages in a review. Published by Writer's Digest Books, an imprint of F+W Publications, Inc., 4700 East Galbraith Road, Cincinnati, Ohio 45236. (800) 289-0963. First edition.

10 09 08 07 06   5 4 3 2 1

Distributed in Canada by Fraser Direct, 100 Armstrong Avenue, George-town, ON, Canada L7G 5S4, Tel: (905) 877-4411. Distributed in the U.K. and Europe by David & Charles, Brunel House, Newton Abbot, Devon, TQ12 4PU, England, Tel: (+44) 1626 323200, Fax: (+44) 1626 323319, E-mail: mail@davidandcharles.co.uk. Distributed in Australia by Capricorn Link, P.O. Box 704, Windsor, NSW 2756 Australia, Tel: (02) 4577-3555.

Library of Congress Cataloging-in-Publication Data

Walton-Porter, Bev.
 Sun signs for writers / by Bev Walton-Porter. -- 1st ed.
    p. cm.
 ISBN 13: 978-1-58297-403-3 (pbk. : alk. paper)
 ISBN 10: 1-58297-403-9
 1. Authorship--Miscellanea. 2. Creation (Literary, artistic, etc.)--Miscellanea.
 3. Zodiac. 4. Astrology. I. Title.
 BF1729.A87W35 2006
 133.5'88--dc22   2006008106

△ Edited by Jane Friedman
ŏ Designed by Grace Ring
)(Production coordinated by Robin Richie

F+W PUBLICATIONS, INC.

acknowledgments

While this book only lists one author on the cover, many people encouraged, motivated, and inspired me to write this book. Special thanks to:

My agent, Meredith Bernstein, for her support and enthusiasm.

Brittany and Jonathan. You are the best kids a mom could ever have.

My twin flame, R. You are the sun, moon, and stars of my life.

My parents, Leo C. Walton Sr. (deceased) and Shirley Walton-Thayer. You believed in me from the beginning.

Friends and writing colleagues—Pat McGrath Avery, Cindy Bement, Sherri Tellez, Joyce Faulkner, Rebecca Forster, Kerri-Leigh Grady, Carolyn Howard-Johnson, Cynthia Kinnecom, Mindy Phillips Lawrence, Stephanie Moyers, Howard Olsen, Venecia Rauls, Jade Walker, and Kai Wilson. Thank you all for your constant friendship and unwavering encouragement.

My sister-in-law, Rita Porter. You are the closest thing to a blood sister I've ever had.

Beth Lilley, who was a consummate writing professional in this world and whose unique flame burns just as bright in the hereafter. I miss you.

Anthony Robbins, who gave me the spark to light the flame.

TaBLe OF COnTenTS

Introduction: Understanding Sun Sign Astrology 1

The Aries Writer (March 21 – April 19) 10
The Taurus Writer (April 20 – May 20) 22
The Gemini Writer (May 21 – June 21) 34
The Cancer Writer (June 22 – July 22) 46
The Leo Writer (July 23 – August 22) 58
The Virgo Writer (August 23 – September 22) 70
The Libra Writer (September 23 – October 22) 78
The Scorpio Writer (October 23 – November 21) 88
The Sagittarius Writer (November 22 – December 21) 98
The Capricorn Writer (December 22 – January 19) 110
The Aquarius Writer (January 20 – February 18) 122
The Pisces Writer (February 19 – March 20) 132

Writers on the Cusp 143
Using Sun Signs to Breathe Life into Your Characters 151

Introduction

What do astrology and writing have in common? More than you
think! *Sun Signs for Writers* is targeted toward readers and writers from the teenage to the elderly who share two characteristics:
First, they consider themselves creative; second, they are drawn
to metaphysical or New Age subjects. While this book is about
both astrology and writing, it blends the subjects in an unusual
way to intrigue, motivate, and inspire readers to know themselves
better not only from an astrological standpoint, but from a creative standpoint as well. At this time, this is the only book on
astrology specifically geared for writers.

What is a sun sign?

Astrology is a complicated discipline. To fully understand the
complexities of astrology, it takes years of study and practice. In
fact, it takes volumes to explain the ins and outs of astrology, so
a complete explanation isn't possible in the limited scope and
space of this book. However, I will give you a basic overview of
astrological sun signs and why your sign influences your writing
life. In this book, you will discover your basic sun sign's tendencies and how you can capitalize on your innate strengths (while
minimizing possible weaknesses) to motivate and inspire you
toward greater writing success. Wouldn't it be interesting to find
out the sun sign of your editor, agent, or writing partner/collabo-
rator (if you have one)?

The following basic explanation of sun signs—and how they relate to you as a person and a writer—will assist those who have never
been exposed to astrology or who have read little more than the
horoscope blurbs found in the morning paper. The zodiac consists

of twelve signs, each related to certain elements, attributes, and animal symbols. These signs (or psychological archetypes) are, in order: Aries, the Ram; Taurus, the Bull; Gemini, the Twins; Cancer, the Crab; Leo, the Lion; Virgo, the Virgin; Libra, the Scales; Scorpio, the Scorpion; Sagittarius, the Centaur (or Archer); Capricorn, the Goat; Aquarius, the Water Bearer; and Pisces, the Fish. Each of these signs inhabits 30 degrees of an astrological chart (which is circular, and thus contains 360 degrees).

Your sun sign is determined by the date you were born (for example, April 11 falls under Aries) and when the sun resides in that sign. The old question *What's your sign?* centers on your sun sign rather than on your moon sign (which is related to what sign the moon was in at the time of your birth) or on your ascendant sign (which is related to what sign was rising at the time of your birth). A person's sun sign defines her general traits, tendencies, and motivations. The focus and motivation for a writer born under one particular sun sign (what I term a *writer sign*) differs from that of a writer born under one of the eleven other writer signs. Simply put, no two writers are ever the same, but it is especially true that a Leo writer is a whole other creature than, say, a Pisces writer.

My relationship with astrology began when I was nine years old. I have studied and been involved with astrology for over thirty years. Not surprisingly, I consult astrological readings on a daily basis. In addition, I often decide when to begin projects based on the planetary influences of any given day, week, month, or year. Eccentric? Perhaps. Entertaining? Always. Celestial matters intrigued me from a young age, and before I became a teenager I attempted to draw my first natal chart by hand—something completed quite easily by a variety of computer programs in this age of technology. A natal chart is a snapshot, if you will, of where the planets were at the exact time you were born—to the minute and by what degree they reside in the house sections of the astrological chart. The time of one's birth and, therefore, the positions of the celestial bodies located in the natal chart, have an impact on the person's astrological-based traits. An astrological natal chart is an individual snapshot, or template, of the underlying influences at the time and place of a person's birth. Slight changes or degrees of position affect how astrological traits are manifested in one's personality. This is why, although there are countless people born under the sun sign of Libra, there are additional aspects in each person's chart that magnify or mute certain general Libran characteristics. Nonetheless, a Libra will always display a general bent toward Libran tendencies, however moderate. Although a natal chart displays general tendencies of the person born at a certain place and time, life experience and a human being's free will dictate that nothing is set in stone in regard to how these tendencies actually do—or do not—play out in life itself. How the traits or characteristics are portrayed (and to what degree) in each person relies on environment, family/social structure, and countless other variables. A person's sun sign is only one section of a larger astrological puzzle.

Qualities of Each Sun Sign

A trio of qualities is associated with each sun sign. Each sign is either masculine or feminine; positive or negative; cardinal, fixed, or mutable. In addition, each sign is associated with either air, earth, fire, or water. What do these qualities mean? A short primer appears below.

Masculine and Feminine Signs

The masculine signs of the zodiac are Aquarius, Aries, Gemini, Leo, Libra, and Sagittarius. The feminine signs are Virgo, Pisces,

Cancer, Scorpio, Taurus, and Capricorn. The masculine or feminine quality of each sign does not relate specifically to gender. Instead, it is a reference to opposites akin to yin and yang in Eastern thought. Signs deemed masculine are seen as more active (yang), while signs deemed feminine are more passive (yin). More active, or masculine signs, are noted as "positive" to indicate a tendency to be more outward and expressive, while those signs listed as passive, or feminine signs, are noted as "negative" to indicate a tendency to be more inward and reserved.

Masculine	Feminine
day	night
light	dark
positive	negative
dry	wet
hot	cold
hard	soft
mental	emotional
loud	quiet
outward	inward

cardinal, fixed, and mutable signs

The cardinal signs of the zodiac are Aries, Cancer, Capricorn, and Libra. They generate action and move forward with blinding energy. They jump-start projects and envision the path from point A to point B with no difficulty. While they make great starters, some of them may need a kick so they'll make it to the end of the road.

The fixed signs are Aquarius, Leo, Scorpio, and Taurus. They sustain momentum and doggedly pursue their quest to cross the finish line of whatever race they undertake. Determination is their virtue, but they may have difficulty keeping their stubborn side under control.

The mutable signs are Sagittarius, Pisces, Gemini, and Virgo. These signs are adaptable and flexible in their approach to life. They roll with the punches and are blessed with ingenuity. On the downside, they sometimes lack consistency and come off as indecisive.

The Four Elements

Each sun sign is also connected to a certain element: air, earth, fire, or water. The traits corresponding to an element correlate to words you might already associate with that particular element. For instance, fire signs burn with frenetic, bold energy. They are assertive, outgoing, and action oriented. Air signs require constant mental stimulation, and their psyches whirl and swoosh like a playful wind. They are intellectual, visionary, and changeable. Water signs are empathic and emotional. They are intense, deep, and inward looking. Finally, earth signs, with their stalwart and reliable natures, are literally the salt of the earth. They are dependable, serious, and practical.

   Fire signs: Aries, Leo, Sagittarius
   Air signs: Aquarius, Libra, Gemini
   Water signs: Cancer, Pisces, Scorpio
   Earth signs: Capricorn, Taurus, Virgo

Typically, fire and air signs mesh well, and earth and water signs are equally compatible. This does not mean that a fire sign will never get along with an earth sign, or that a water sign will never make fast friends with an air sign. (Keep in mind that the sun sign is only one facet of a person's character, so the sign and planetary combinations in an individual's chart can lead to interesting connections with others, even those not usually compatible.) Understanding the general characteristics of a certain sun sign can lead to valuable insight into yourself and others; if you understand the astrological basis for your Cancer friend's approaches to life and writing, you'll find it much easier to reach a meeting of the minds.

THE RULING PLANETS

Each sun sign is associated with a ruling planet. The sun signs, their ruling planets, and the influences of each planet are as follows:

SUN SIGN	RULING PLANET
Aries	Mars
Taurus	Venus
Gemini	Mercury
Cancer	Moon
Leo	Sun
Virgo	Mercury
Libra	Venus
Scorpio	Pluto
Sagittarius	Jupiter
Capricorn	Saturn
Aquarius	Uranus
Pisces	Neptune

Sun. The Sun, as a ruling planet, centers on the ego, will, and leadership. Its influence highlights such qualities as confidence, extraversion, and power. The Sun's influences may also lead to qualities such as egocentrism, stubbornness, and elitism.

Moon. Moon is the planet tied to emotions, subconscious, and reflection. Lunar influences of this planet may include protectiveness, empathy, and domesticity. Alternatively, the moon as a ruling planet may also bring oversensitivity, withdrawal, and moodiness.

Mercury. Mercury is known as the planet of communication, thought, and academic pursuits. Influences of this planet include restlessness, logic, and curiosity. Mercury's influence may also manifest itself in nervousness, emotional detachment, and superficiality.

Venus. Venus bestows a planetary influence that touts balance, reflection, and harmony. The hallmarks of its influence include artistic leanings, diplomacy, and pleasure. In addition, Venus may also highlight qualities such as vacillation, hesitancy, and avoidance.

Mars. Mars is known as an active, bold, and action-oriented ruling planet. Its influence is one that is aggressive, enterprising, and forward-moving. Its force can also be argumentative, warlike, and combative.

Jupiter. Jupiter is associated with justice, luck, and independence. This ruling planet is associated with philosophy, religion, and justice. Jupiter may also bring about overconfidence, narcissism, and carelessness.

Saturn. Saturn is known as a planet entrenched in conservatism, realism, and caution. This ruling planet imposes order, structure, and discipline. Saturn's influences may also manifest in rigidity, close-mindedness, and stagnation.

Uranus. Uranus is a ruling planet that highlights science, innovation, and the unconventional. As a ruling planet, common keywords include freedom, justice, and progress. Uranus's influences may also bring aloofness, rebelliousness, and detachment.

Neptune. Neptune's planetary influences include compassion, humanitarianism, and illusion. This ruling planet may also be associated with utopia, divinity, and sensitivity. Neptune's planetary touch may also produce zealotry, disassociation, and neurosis.

Pluto. Pluto is the planet often associated with life-altering change, destruction, and mystery. This outer ruling planet's influences include rebirth, exposure, and power. Pluto can also signify the hidden, sexuality, and courage.

HOW TO USE THIS BOOK

The purpose of this book is threefold. First, it will teach you the foundational characteristics of your zodiacal sun sign. It will touch on aspects of your sun sign that may make you a stronger writer, while cautioning you about sun sign traits that may hinder your progress. Because astrological influences are specific to your exact date and time of birth, you may find that you possess some writer sign traits, but not all of them.

Second, this book will offer creative-writing exercises designed for each writer sign's tendencies. By working in harmony with the aspects these exercises are designed around, you can explore your inner muse and connect with her. This connection can result in a deeper recognition of the gifts within you. The exercises may also help you strengthen weak spots. They will help you stretch your boundaries and hone your innate talents and abilities. Complete the writing exercises under your sun sign and then branch out and explore the exercises under other writer sign profiles—just for fun!

Third, this book will introduce you to a new tool for developing characters: creating personalities based on sun sign profiles. When developing characters for a fictional story or novel, it's important to avoid cardboard characters—characters that seem flat and artificial. Your readers want realistic people they can believe in. You can find discussions of the many tactics for mastering characterization in countless books on writing, but in this book, I will show you a unique and creative way to build the perfect foundation for believable characters. Once you have read the chapter on building celestial-based characters, you will be able to craft the perfect physical, mental, emotional, and spiritual person to suit your story needs. By using astrological archetypes as a tool, you can develop believable personas driven by logical motivations, realistic flaws, and genuine internal conflict.

A FINAL WORD

When it comes to astrology, skeptics abound. Perhaps you are one of them. For the time being, put aside your preconceived notions and consider, as a writer, how astrology can be used as an interesting and useful tool for better understanding human nature and, most importantly, understanding how your characters might act if they happened to be born under a certain zodiacal sign. Each sign serves as an archetype of human behavior, with its own positive and negative qualities—a sort of yin and yang of personality. By using the pure astrological types, you can mold and shape realistic people to inhabit your stories. What's more, once you become familiar with each sign type, you can mix and match aspects of two or three signs together to represent the influences of not only the sun sign, but the moon and ascendant signs as well.

This book gives you another unique option for fleshing out your characters, and offers strategies for your quest to produce your best possible written work. While you may insist you're not the typical Capricorn writer as described in this book, chances are you'll find one or two traits that ring true—even if in only a small way. So dive in and explore fully the various writer types, try the writing exercises on for size, and delve into the world of celestial character building. The journey may be new and different to you, but I suspect you'll find it both enlightening and entertaining in the end!

The difference between fiction and reality? Fiction has to make sense.
—TOM CLANCY

Key personality traits: ambitious, competitive, tenacious, head-strong

Symbol: the Ram

Element: fire

Ruling planet: Mars

Qualities: positive, masculine, cardinal

MARCH 21–APRIL 19

Aries

writers are the go-getters of the zodiac. Dynamic by nature, they are assertive pioneers. As the first sign of the zodiac, they are natural leaders and never shy away from a challenge. Complicated or daring writing projects that might make other writers shudder in their shoes are nothing more than an attractive dare to those born under the symbol of the Ram. Aries writers laugh at intimidation of any kind; they jump right in, in their customary bold and self-assured fashion, then proceed to show everyone else how the job is done. Their direct personality is sometimes seen as pushy by others, but the truth is, when Aries writers have a goal in mind and see an open path, they will pursue it with as much gusto as they can muster. Moderation is a word foreign to their vocabularies—and a concept foreign to their lives!

Blunt and forceful, Aries writers would do well to learn how to slow down a bit, to take a more measured view of their course, and to listen to the opinions and advice of others. Like the Ram, they can be hard-headed at times, and this can be their downfall. Their minds are quick and their intellects sharp, but it wouldn't hurt them to sit back and consider other perspectives once in a while—especially when those other perspectives come from editors or agents. Finally, not everyone moves at their breakneck pace, so they should cultivate patience for others who aren't as lightning-quick. The publishing industry may not move as fast as they'd like, and waiting weeks (or months) for the response to a query may drive them up the wall. They need to calm down, take a deep breath, and keep their minds off the waiting game by getting involved in a variety of alternative projects.

Four Foolproof Ways Aries Can Smash Writer's Block

1. Yes, it can happen to you. Aries writers *never* get writer's block, right? Wrong! While you are on high speed most of the time, on occasion you might find yourself stalled despite your best efforts. If you hit a dead end on your novel or short story and you can't seem to get past the hump, switch gears and work on one of the many other projects you're likely to have in your stable. It's unlikely that you don't have another writing project raring to go, but if you don't, create one. Don't think about markets, don't think about publication, don't think about pay rates—just write. The goal here is to get the ink flowing smoothly again. Once the words are rushing like a stream, switch to your previous work and let 'er rip.

2. Develop patience. Patience isn't on the top of the list of Aries virtues. You are all about action and results, not patience and persistence. You want to get published, and you want to get published *now*, not tomorrow or in the distant future. There are articles and novels out there waiting to be written—and by you, no less! You've got a fire in your belly, and when the words don't come as easily as you believe they should, you become frustrated and disgusted with yourself. On occasion, you also get miffed with others around you. Getting worked up over temporary glitches with your muse won't help the situation, Aries, it will only exacerbate it. Don't magnify the pressure of writer's block by feeding the problem with anger and frustration. Of course you're anxious and ready to get going again, but like it or not, you may need to take a breather and calm down a bit before heading back to the keyboard.

3. Conquer the world another day. In your typical Aries fashion, when you decide you want to write, you will most likely want to conquer the publishing world, beginning at the top. Learning the ropes takes time and discipline. Not everything you write has to be targeted toward the best or most prestigious magazine in the business—at least not yet. Putting yourself under pressure to churn out work for the cream of the crop at the beginning of your writing career may put the brakes on your creativity and prevent you from making headway when you want it the most. Give yourself time to practice and to find your own rhythm, voice, and style before you lunge headlong into the deep end.

4. Court your muse. All work and no play makes Aries one grumpy and stopped-up writer. If that business article isn't coming along as you planned, and you're tired of staring at the blank screen, break the monotony by grabbing your muse by the hand and heading out for a different sort of journey. Haven't written poetry in a while? Time to take a detour and indulge. Never write fiction? Maybe it's time you gave it a whirl. *But I have paid writing I must do!* you grouse. Understandable, but when you're stuck in neutral and revving your engine to no avail, it's time to kick into a higher gear and go off-road. Consider this off-road journey more than a diversion; it's fuel for your writing engine.

Dealing with Rejection

Rejection is a bitter pill to swallow for most Aries writers. Not because you question your abilities after a rejection, but because you pride yourself on doing your best. When you expect to succeed and don't, the perceived failure sticks in your craw. *How can they not see my brilliance and talent?* you may wonder. Here is a nugget of truth no one may have told you before: Your work will get rejected no matter how well you write. Sometimes the piece is wrong, sometimes the timing is wrong, sometimes the planetary alignment is wrong. Insert any and all other reasons (real or imagined) in the previous sentence, but you'll have to deal with one incontrovertible fact—rejection happens, and it will happen to you whether you like it or not!

The best medicine for Aries when dealing with rejection is to learn how to distribute your substantial energy over a variety of projects. Once the rejections hit, their impact will be lessened; you'll be too busy wrestling with your other ten million projects to pay them much attention. Instead of fuming over the latest editorial rebuff, channel that emotion into a new query or proposal.

rejection do's and don'ts

- **Do listen to others' opinions.** You're a take-charge person with more leadership ability in your little finger than most people have in their whole body (or so you'd like to believe). Most of the time you probably *do* know best, but can it hurt to solicit advice from others on occasion? Find a trustworthy scribe you respect and ask if she will look over your work and offer constructive input. While you may not agree with the person's initial assessment of your writing, don't be too quick to dismiss the other point of view. Listen without prejudice and consider what suggestions may improve your chances of publication. Another set of eyes can be beneficial when you're too close to your own work. You may receive valuable feedback you can use to tweak your submission for maximum salability.

- **Don't take rejection as a personal affront.** Aries souls are born headstrong and proud—good qualities to be sure—but too much of this good thing can occasionally lead to arrogance. Your story might be the cream of the crop, but even the best stories don't always fit the scheme of a particular publication. A pass on your work isn't necessarily a slight. Never confront an editor or become defensive. Questioning an editor's decision will put you on the shortlist of writers *not* to hire in the future. Making waves will only result in harm to you.

· **Do keep current guidelines handy.** Editors change houses so often that it can seem like they're engaged in their own game of musical chairs. With new editors often come new or improved writer's guidelines. Keep a database of guidelines and update them on a regular basis. One of the quickest ways to rejection is assuming you know what a publication needs instead of checking the current list of editorial needs and wants. If your guidelines are months or years old, it's time to update your records. The more familiar you are with a publisher's or magazine's guidelines, the better chance you have of nailing an assignment.

· **Don't bend the rules.** It might be tempting for you to break with protocol (after all, you've probably been doing it most of your life), but when it comes to dealing with editors, publishers, and agents, one of the fastest ways to get your work rejected is to blatantly circumvent the rules. There is no shortcut through certain formalities of the publishing industry, so be prepared to follow standard procedures in order to leave the best impression.

GIVING anD RECEIVING CRITICISM

Ever heard the phrase *cut to the chase*? That describes the Aries approach to offering assessments of others' writing. Aries is all about action and less about contemplation. They size up situations, see what needs to be done, and then do it. The ram can spot a split infinitive from ten paces, and they can transform passive sentences to active ones in the blink of an eye. Aries know a good read when they see one, and what's more, they know instinctively what other authors should do to pull in their readers. Their method of delivery, however, leaves much to be desired. The whys and hows of revision may be obvious, but writers on the receiving end of an Aries appraisal may need in-depth explanation. Although it may be clear to an Aries what you should do to polish your piece, don't be afraid to ask for further discussion on the subject. The ram loves to give advice and is flattered by it; he won't take offense to your probing questions or suggestions for elaboration on how to improve your writing.

When it's an Aries's turn to be on the receiving side of criticism, they aren't nearly as receptive. Aries hates rejection in all its forms, and they will avoid it at all costs. The idea of missing the mark on any project fills Aries with anxiety—but they won't let others know that unless they absolutely have to. While they may come off as a tad arrogant, deep inside they cannot stand the slightest hint of failure. Be sure to let them know suggestions about their writing style is not a direct attack on them. Let Aries know, unequivocally, that as a fellow scribe you want them to succeed and they should view constructive criticism as a tool for vaulting themselves closer to publication rather than as a challenge to their ego. Remind them of this: If other writers didn't feel their writing was worthy of comment, they wouldn't go to the trouble to offer insight into Aries's words.

10 PATHS TO PUBLICATION FOR ARIES

1. Fill 'er up. If you write for magazines, keep in mind that, these days, magazine readers want short, bite-sized bits of helpful information that make their lives easier on a day-to-day basis. Think beyond the obvious 2,000-word article and consider penning miniature tips and fillers for a variety of publications. A 100-word filler can easily net you fifty dollars or more, so don't dismiss the publication potential of these shorter snippets. Writing short can lead to a long and steady stream of payments.

2. Voice your opinion. Need a point of view on any topic under the sun? Aries will always have one, regardless of the subject matter. The Ram is never wishy-washy and is all too happy to express her stance on any issue, so op-ed pieces can be a market worth exploring. Op-ed pieces range from 500 to 800 words in most cases, and are featured in newspapers and magazines around the world. To get the feel for an op-ed piece, grab a print newspaper or access an online version of your local community paper. Although you'll find that many op-eds are penned by experts, such experts don't have the market cornered. Get in touch with your local newspaper editor and request the guidelines for submitting op-eds. Once you have some experience under your belt, go after larger publications in other regions.

3. Spin fact into fiction. Get in the habit of clipping any and all interesting bits of news and information you can get your hands on. Start a series of file folders, each labeled according to subject matter, then snip and file articles, reports, and features that pique your interest. While you may not have a specific use for the clips right away, you never know when a current event will spark a new idea that will lead to a salable piece of work. Go through your clip folders once every month, and use them as launch tools for query ideas. Don't just collect the clips and forget about them; actively use the information to create unique pitches.

4. Get specific. Before mailing off a query, be sure you have the correct information on the editor who'll receive your work. If you cannot locate current masthead details, call the editorial offices and ask to whom you should send your submission. Be polite and squelch the urge to expand the conversation beyond requesting the name and mailing address of the appropriate editor. Get the required information, offer a few sincere words of thanks, then politely hang up.

5. Pep up your pitch. Aries are great at selling themselves and others, so let that talent show through. You come across as confident and fiery. Channel your knock-'em-dead energy into writing pitches and cover letters filled with dynamic, at-tention-grabbing words and active verbs instead of dull adverbs and adjectives. With careful attention and the right choice of words, you'll turn an average query into an irresistible invita-tion no editor can resist.

6. Cater to your editor. Rams are brimming with pride, and they don't automatically bestow respect on just anyone. However, in the publishing business, you'll need to keep your ego in check. Remind yourself that how you treat your editors affects whether they'll use your work again. Don't balk at suggested changes or argue with editorial policy—ever. There are a million other writers out there waiting to take your place, so strive to remain pleasant and receptive even in times of disagreement. The fact is, writers who are easier to work with have a better chance of landing repeat assignments.

7. Compare markets. Just as you comparison shop for the best deal in a grocery store, so should you actively compare compet-ing markets before you decide to query them. Weigh factors such as pay scale, rights requested, percentage of freelance content, publication timeline, quality, and when payment is made (on publication or on acceptance) before judging the best place to make your pitch. While the aim for beginning writers is to rack up credits for your writing résumé, you also need to remember to look out for your own best interests.   Experienced writers who have a track record of publishing credits will focus on writing for income, so comparing details of potential markets is even more important.

8. Emphasize your entrepreneurial spirit! You have a sharp mind for business and know how to relate to those who are self-employed or who work in unconventional careers (because, hey, you're part of the group!). Use your savvy business acumen to write for publications that cater to nontraditional workers. You have the knack for nailing this lucrative market, which features topics ranging from how-to articles to interviews with movers and shakers in the entrepreneurial world.

9. Motivate others. Self-improvement offers infinite writing opportunities. As an eloquent and inspirational speaker by nature, you know how to motivate with your words. Weave your wisdom into written form and target publications geared toward ambitious readers looking to get ahead.

10. Patience is a virtue! Aries is charged up and always ready to go. However, the rest of the world isn't as hyped up as you are, and editorial decisions aren't made at the speed of light. You'll need to work on your tolerance level and develop patience with others who might be less than gung ho for your project. By having many assignments going at once, you'll keep your attention focused elsewhere, and your internal timer won't drive you quite so mad. Remember: Everything in due time, Aries.

Exercises for Aries

If the rest of the world burns with a steady flame, then Aries writers are the raging wildfires of the world. Because you are always the first out of the gate and competitive to the end, no one will ever accuse you of not putting 100 percent into your efforts. Stoke your internal creative fire with these writing exercises tailored specifically for the Ram in you.

1. Support the underdog. You're attracted to any story that centers on a less-than-fortunate character and how she triumphs over terrible odds in order to come out on top. Imagine a scenario featuring a character who is in dire straits, yet who persists in her quest to triumph, then step into her fictional life. Compose diary entries based on the worst possible episode of that character's life, detailing the events of those trying days as well as how the person reacted and what emotions emerged from such unfortunate events. By the end of the series of entries, show how your character resolves to take the steps needed to solve her problems and triumph over adversity.

2. Hone your powers of persuasion. Pretend you are the CEO of a start-up company that's in need of capital. In less than two hours, you're scheduled to give a speech to possible investors for your new company. Your presentation will be broadcast via closed-circuit television across the globe. Pen a short speech that will persuade the investors to explore your company further and invest in its future.

FAMOUS ARIES WRITERS

March 26, 1942	Erica Jong
March 26, 1943	Bob Woodward
April 2, 1805	Hans Christian Andersen
April 3, 1783	Washington Irving
April 4, 1928	Maya Angelou
April 5, 1920	Arthur Hailey
April 9, 1821	Charles Baudelaire
April 12, 1916	Beverly Cleary
April 12, 1947	Tom Clancy
April 12, 1949	Scott Turow
April 13, 1909	Eudora Welty
April 15, 1843	Henry James

Don't talk about it, just write. And read widely, and think about what you read. And let grammar, spelling, and punctuation enter your life.

—TERRY PRATCHETT

Key personality traits: focused, steadfast, determined, earthy

Symbol: the Bull

Element: earth

Ruling planet: Venus

Qualities: negative, fixed, feminine

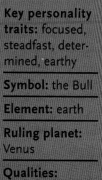

APRIL 20–MAY 20

Taurus

writers are deliberate and hard-working. These scribes will labor patiently and steadily to reach their goals and have little propensity toward distraction. Like the sturdy and purposeful Bull that symbolizes this writer sign, no matter how adverse the conditions or how challenging the task may be, the patient Taurus writer will take on the yoke of responsibility and carry it with grace and dignity. Practical and focused at the core, these writers may need a nudge or two to get started, but once they begin their journey, they are one of the most reliable finishers of the zodiac. In addition, Taurus writers are tuned in to the sensual side of life with all its smells, tastes, textures, sights, and sounds. This sensuality carries over well to their writing endeavors. Look for vivid descriptions in their work; they will no doubt transport their readers into the world of their characters with lush descriptions of atmosphere and setting.

Those born under the sign of Taurus are happiest when their circumstances are predictable. Therefore, their charge is to learn how to stretch their horizons a bit and not be afraid to strike out into new territory in their writing pursuits. Taurus writers may find more comfort in staying in one genre or tackling the same old topics (or derivatives of those topics), but by limiting their vision, they may be cutting off possible sources of future publication. Ruled by the planet Venus, they are attracted to romance and all its aspects. It's no surprise to find many Taurus writers working in the romance genre.

Four Foolproof Ways Taurus Can Smash Writer's Block

1. **Hit the right note.** Taurus natives are musically inclined. If they do not have a wonderful voice, then at the minimum they

have a fine appreciation for various types of music. Like music, writing possesses a distinct rhythm. Block occurs when your mind is temporarily out of sync and you can't seem to hit the right note in your prose, poetry, or nonfiction. When the muse refuses to cooperate, push away your pen and fire up the CD player or the radio. Immerse yourself in a variety of music. Sit back, close your eyes, and imagine how you would describe each song in words to a person who hasn't heard it before. Don't think you can? Give it a try. If you translated the rhythm and harmony into nouns, verbs, and adjectives, how would the translated arrangement read? There are beats in writing, just as there are beats in instrumental compositions. By viewing the act of writing as a rhythmic exercise of creation, you can use music to tear down superficial barriers.

2. Take it outdoors. Inspiration can occur almost anywhere. Something magical happens to Taurus writers when they have close encounters with Mother Nature. When you find that your creative well is running dry and imagination is at an all-time low, grab a notebook and head for the outdoors. If you live in a city, find a park with wide expanses of green grass and tall shade trees. If you're lucky enough to reside in the country, discover a quiet spot where you are surrounded by nothing more than the soughing of wind through the trees (or wheat fields, if you live in the Midwest). Breathe deeply, connect with your senses, and record how your mind, body, and soul react to being in this place at this moment. Jot down words, phrases, sentences—whether or not they make sense. Give yourself permission to muse for the sake of musing.

3. Break it down. You've finally decided to write the Great American Novel. Now you find yourself stalled. As much as you want to write this book, the right first sentence escapes you. Writing a

100,000-word novel is no easy task, and the very idea of embarking on such a gargantuan journey is enough to rein in a writer before he even gets out of the starting gate. How can you work through your fear and start off on the right foot? Break up the task into manageable steps, then reward yourself as you complete each level. Tell yourself you will write for a certain time each day without regard to word or page counts. The first week, strive for a half-hour of nonstop writing time each day. After seven days of sticking to your goal, treat yourself to a small gift or outing to celebrate. The following week, increase your writing time by fifteen to thirty minutes more, then select an even larger reward for your accomplishments. Increase your writing time in small increments every week until you are working at a steady maximum you find comfortable. Before long, the writing will flow with less effort and the pages will appear like magic.

4. **Revamp your workspace.** The Venusian influence of your sign dictates that, for you to do your best work as a writer, your workspace must be comfortable and appealing to all your senses. After all, you Taurus writers can't be expected to create in a bland atmosphere, can you? Decorate your computer desk with colorful knickknacks, inspirational quote calendars, plants, and scented potpourri. Hang inexpensive art on the walls and be sure to keep a music source nearby to quench your musical thirst on occasion (or, if you aren't too distracted by it, to play soft background music as you write).

DEALING WITH REJECTION

Patience is difficult for some, but it is ingrained in the Bull. While you've got more patience in your pinky finger than any other sign has in his entire body, it's still important for you to see marked progress on your road to publication. While one rejection might not set you offtrack, a handful could cause you to derail (albeit temporarily). Resolute in your drive to see your words in print, you'll continue to plod along in your customary Taurus way—but eventually you'll expect favorable results. You understand that pitfalls are common during the process of trying to get published, and your steady nature guarantees you will overcome them if you don't psyche yourself out. Control your emotional reaction to the word *no*, and you'll be that much closer to hitting your mark.

The best way for Taurus writers to combat rejection is to keep track of what you have accomplished rather than concentrating on what you haven't. Once you get going, you'll stay on track and keep your drive alive—unless you become discouraged over perceived failures. Count the small victories, not just the big misses. Did you submit three more queries than last week? That's progress, Taurus! Refuse to dwell on setbacks, and keep pressing forward. If you slow down or stop, it'll take twice as much energy to get you going again.

Rejection do's and don'ts

- **Do seek comfort in your persistence.** Even in the face of repeated rejections, Taurus natives need to accentuate the positive and lessen the sting of the negative. Instead of taking note of how many articles haven't been accepted over the past year, zero in on the number of submissions you've sent out or how many words you've written overall. Maybe you haven't sold your book manuscript yet, but finishing it is a feat worthy of praise! Remember, most people never attempt to write because it's *hard work*. Give yourself credit where credit is due, then keep plugging away.

- **Don't lose momentum.** When the going gets tough, you're apt to slow down or grind to a screeching halt. The problem is that it takes a long time to get you motivated to begin again after a setback. It's important for you to follow up each rejection with a counteraction. Find another market, rewrite your query or embark on another project. Whatever you decide, the key is to keep the momentum going so you won't stall!

- **Do be gracious.** Upon receiving a rejection from an editor, respond with a quick note thanking the editor for his time and letting him know that, while you're disappointed your piece didn't work for him, you appreciate his consideration. While some writers feel this is a wasted effort, the truth is that your thank-you note will make you stand out as an appreciative writer. The next time your name comes across that editor's desk, he might remember you took that extra step, and he might give your submission a closer look.

- **Don't ever give up on a market.** Sure, you've submitted what you believe is your best work to a certain magazine more times than you can count. Now you're ready to cross it off your list and sprint to what you hope will be greener pastures. Not so quick! It's easy to dismiss a publication when you've struck out scores of times, but maybe your best bet is to set that market on the shelf for a while instead of abandoning it outright. Editors come and go at publications, and content needs can change. What won't sell today might appeal in the future. Never cross off a market completely. Put it on hold and revisit it in the future.

GIVING and RECEIVING CRITICISM

Taurus natives won't hesitate to offer sound advice that is both practical and concrete. Chances are, they have read a variety of genres and styles and are familiar with all of them. Fair and honest in their assessments, they are all about quality. When a fellow scribe needs help with revisions, Taurus will take as much care with the piece as they would if it were their own handiwork. While Taurus won't hold back on needed criticism, the Bull will take care to deliver it in a constructive and clear manner. Any advice they provide for others will be solid, practical, and on-target for publication. Grounded as they are, Taurus won't provide you with pie-in-the-sky compliments or puffery; instead, they will deliver a no-nonsense assessment of your writing and will help you doggedly pursue the path that will help you reach your stated goals.

Taurus is much better at doling out criticism than they are at taking it. They must learn to balance their eagerness to give with their willingness to receive. Taurus writers like to do it their way. They will appreciate your guidance, but may let you know they still see their way as the best approach. Other writers will need to prove that their suggestions are worthy and practical before Taurus will consider changing one single word on the page. Even then, they are not likely to abandon the original intent. It's not that Taurus believes you or others offer terrible advice on how to revise; it's that they are sure they know how to patch up writing faux pas better than anyone else. Be tactful and deliberate when you offer the Bull criticism and realize that while they are not as outwardly resistant as Aries can be, on the inside they are ten times more immovable—bullish in their resolve. Remind them that if they can't bring themselves to make giant changes based on others' critiques, they should at least try to budge a tiny bit in the spirit of being gracious and receptive.

10 PATHS TO PUBLICATION FOR TAURUS

1. **Shake up your old query routine.** Look for new ways of making contacts with up-and-coming publications, and be the first

out of the gate to contact them and ask if they need the services of a professional freelancer. Provide samples of various types of writing you've done, and offer to pen a sample piece according to their instructions.

2. Never beg an editor. Writing is a business, not a charity. Editors are people, but they won't be swayed by sob stories or dramatic overtures. Steer clear of amateurish pleas such as *I've been writing five years and never been published; won't you* please *give me a chance?* Editors don't want to know that your parents believe you're the next J.K. Rowling, either. They *do* want professional writers who can furnish them with error-free, interesting content. Amateurs need not apply.

3. Indulge in passions of the palate. Those born under the influence of the planet Venus love the good life and everything that it brings—especially delicious food and drink. There is a plethora of magazines and cookbooks in the world; why not take advantage and share your own domestic contributions? Taurus writers can flaunt their kitchen expertise—from preparing the perfect pasta to mastering meringue—and rake in article acceptances at the same time.

4. Get lyrical. Music is entrenched in the souls of the majority of Taurus writers, so if you've never thought of trying your hand at songwriting, it's past time you did. You know all about the rhythm found in music and in words, so writing lyrics should be second nature to you. Peruse books and Web sites for professional songwriters and lyricists and learn where and how to submit your compositions for pay. And don't *ever* pay someone to read your lyrics or to publish them. Legitimate companies pay *you* to publish your work—not the other way around.

5. Make your readers feel at home. You may not be the next Martha Stewart, but most Taurus writers are suckers for the creature comforts of home. When it comes to interior design or decorating on a dime, you've got hundreds of tips and tricks to share with readers. Boost your credits with how-to articles for publications devoted to the joys of domesticity. Whether the topic is planning the perfect party or wallpapering like a pro, you'll no doubt have it covered.

6. Be stubborn. Those born under the sign of the Bull are noted for their wide stubborn streak. While this might not be a good thing in all cases, when it comes to writing, it can be beneficial. Unlike some other signs, you won't give up at the first sign of rejection; instead, you'll plod along until you find a way to break through the wall in front of you. One of the top principles in getting published is to never give up, so use your naturally unbending will to push through any barriers you encounter.

7. Flaunt your green thumb. Most Taurus natives love the outdoors as well as landscaping and gardening. If you don't have a garden, it's likely you tend various plants and herbs in your home. If your local paper doesn't have a gardening column, why not suggest one? You don't have to be an expert or have an advanced degree in botany to qualify as a regional correspondent. Contact the community extension offices of local universities and inquire about opportunities to write for their agriculture or gardening publications. Once you've gotten your feet wet, move on to querying larger specialty markets.

8. Stay active. Make your writing snappier—and more purchase worthy—by minding your active and passive voice. When you write in active voice, the subject of your sentence acts upon something; when you write in passive voice, the subject of your sentence is acted upon by some other person or thing. *Joe caught the ball* is active, while *The ball was caught by Joe* is passive. While there are instances in which passive voice is acceptable, you should use active voice whenever possible. Your writing will flow better and put a smile on your editor's face at the same time!

9. Mind your marks. When it comes to writing, little things count. Even a tiny mistake—such as a misused apostrophe—can make a difference. Apostrophe misuse can brand you as a novice, so learn the correct way to use this important punctuation mark. Properly used to show possession (as in *Katie's*) or to replace missing letters in a contraction (as in *can't*), apostrophes are often used incorrectly to indicate plurals (as in *carrot's for sale*). Not sure how to use the apostrophe? Grab some books from the library or look online for Web sites devoted to proper punctuation. If you think this discussion of apostrophes is much ado about nothing, tell that to the Apostrophe Protection Society (www.apostrophe.fsnet. co.uk); to them, apostrophe misuse is serious business indeed. It should be for you, too.

10. Cut your queries. It's tempting to bang out a five-page query letter so you can include everything you know about a subject to interest an editor, but don't do it. As much as it'll hurt, cut your query length down to one page, no more. Editors are deluged with more mail than they can ever hope to sort through in a single week, so make your point quickly. Give them the basics of your article: why it fits with their publication, how long it will be, why you're the person to write it, and how your article differs from others on the subject. Hook them early and have them asking to see more.

Exercises for Taurus

Taurus writers are methodical, steady scribes who move forward with persistence until they reach their end goal. They are attracted to romance, music, beauty, and comfort. These writing exercises will assist you in connecting with the sensual, creative side of your muse.

1. Describe your favorite dessert. Pick your favorite dessert, then imagine you have arrived in a foreign country and have been invited to dine with top dignitaries from that nation. They ask you to share with them one food from your native land. They insist you describe to their head chef what the food is, how it is prepared, and what it tastes like. If you had to detail your favorite dessert to someone who lives in a different country and who may not have the same types of food as you do, how would you describe the essence, flavor, and composition of your favorite dish? First, write out the details as accurately as possible using simple and concrete words. Next, write a second description using nothing but abstract words and expressive phrases.

2. **Consider the word** *beauty* **and what it means to you.** Is beauty merely in the *eye* of the beholder? How would beauty taste, feel, sound, or smell if it were in the tongue, fingertips, ears, or nose of the beholder? List each of the senses, then take no more than five minutes to explain how beauty relates to each sense, giving an example for each.

FAMOUS TAURUS WRITERS

April 21, 1816	Charlotte Brontë
April 22, 1943	Janet Evanovich
April 24, 1940	Sue Grafton
April 28, 1948	Terry Pratchett
May 1, 1923	Joseph Heller
May 2, 1941	Stephen J. Cannell
May 5, 1933	Barbara Taylor Bradford
May 8, 1937	Thomas Pynchon
May 8, 1940	Peter Benchley
May 9, 1860	J.M. Barrie
May 17, 1946	F. Paul Wilson

The use of language is all we have
to pit against death and silence.
—Joyce Carol Oates

Key personality traits: communicative, flexible, inquisitive, versatile

Symbol: the Twins

Element: air

Ruling planet: Mercury

Qualities: positive, masculine, mutable

may 21–june 21

Geminis are the great communicators of the zodiac. They are social, inquisitive, talkative, and intellectual.

Geminis are the great communicators of the zodiac. They are social, inquisitive, talkative, and intellectual. They make great journalists because they are flexible and objective—you can send them on an assignment across the globe on a moment's notice, and they won't balk. Geminis are terrific at brainstorming and usually have a million ideas for stories and articles buzzing around in their head at any given moment. Gemini writers are also adept at multitasking, and it's nothing to find them working on several projects at once; what's more, they'll plunge into something new at the drop of a hat.

Although the social Gemini is blessed with the gift of gab, she faces a big challenge when it comes to focus and follow-through. Those born under the sign of the Twins are admirable starters but questionable finishers. It's not that they aren't good enough— they are some of the most talented scribes in this universe and beyond! It's more that they become bored easily and are eager to move on to the next big thing. To a Gemini, life experience is a smorgasbord of tasty delights. She would rather move along to the next delectable entrée than waste time hovering over one dish for too long. Given the Gemini writer's tendency to stray once she loses enthusiasm for a task, it's important for her to find writing projects that will hold her interest.

Four Foolproof Ways Gemini Can Smash Writer's Block

1. **Shift your brain into overdrive.** Geminis are the natural brainstormers of the zodiac. Get a group of writers together, and it will be a rare event when the Twin-spirited one among them isn't tossing out handfuls of new and innovative plot twists on a split second's notice. However, even the most inspired scribes

find themselves in the black hole of inertia on occasion. To keep those ideas flowing and the writing humming right along, tap into your brainstorming abilities and exercise your talent on a daily basis. Just as physical exercise keeps your body's muscles toned and at the ready, mental exercises keep you sharp, agile, and ready to attack the page.

2. Keep silent. Writers born under the sign of the Twins love to talk (boy, do they!). Born with the gift of verbal expression and quick to use it, you should avoid talking so much that you cheat yourself out of potential material. Learn to keep your inspiration close to the vest, and curb the urge to gab, blather, and share every little tidbit that resides in your head. Although communication is your specialty, you must learn to channel your energies in the proper way—through the pen and not through your tongue! Quiet down, zip your lip, and do your talking on the page.

3. Go deep. As a Gemini native, you are quick in thought and speech. Others may see you as superficial and more into logic than complex, profound feeling. This is an unfair assessment, since you can be as intense as any other writer sign. The difference is that you're selective about who you share your feelings with. You like to keep it light and airy. While this is admirable most of the time, in order to uncover new avenues of creativity, you must delve into the core of your creative being. Excavate deep connections from your emotional history by selecting an isolated moment from your past, and then writing about how you reacted on all sense levels during that moment in time. What did you see, hear, smell, taste, touch during that particular moment? Find concrete words to describe these sensations from your past and log them in a diary or writing journal. Go beyond the intellect and plug into the seminal feel of moods and emotions. Keep your muse nourished by allowing her to feed off those emotions.

GEMINI

4. Change your perspective. When you stall—which doesn't happen often—it's in your frenetic nature to move on to another project. While moving on is good advice for other signs, it can spell disaster for the Gemini. Why? Because you, dear Gemini, have a million ideas as it is, and although you are an excellent initiator, you need extra help to finish. If you get tripped up on writing a short story and you're not sure where to go next, your first instinct will be to pounce on one of the gazillion other ideas you have floating around. Trouble is, if you do that, you probably won't go back to your previous project for a very long time—if ever. Stay with the current writing task by forcing yourself to look at it from a different angle. The new perspective will get you fired up again and get you back into action!

DEALING WITH REJECTION

If your ego is challenged by a rejection, the sting never lasts long—you won't allow it. You're optimistic most of the time, and it's not rejection per se that gets you down. What floors you is the feeling of running in one place and not making headway as quickly as you'd like. A certain amount of frustration is to be expected when your work is sent back to you, unpublished. But don't blow the event out of proportion.

When the going gets rough, your first instinct is often to leave the game altogether. The thing is, you'll never find smooth sailing in the writing biz. It's best for you to prepare for the inevitable and learn how to weather the many storms you're likely to come up against. Persistence and tenacity are what you need to shoot for, dear Gemini. How can you ever know sweet victory if you abandon projects that have been passed over once or twice? The answer is, you can't. One rejection does not make for failure, so you must get back on that horse and ride it again (and again and again). This takes patience you may not have. But consider persistence and tenacity to be qualities necessary for development and ultimate success.

Rejection Do's and Don'ts

- **Do work on your stick-to-itiveness.** You may have to revise and reframe an article numerous times in order to sell it. Picture in your mind how your finished project will read once it's complete. Go through the whole experience—publication, reviews, accolades—so you can feel it. By envisioning the success of a finished novel or story, you will find the motivation you need to keep going until you reach the finish line. Cultivate your enthusiasm for the project and motivate yourself to stay with the task by reminding yourself of the sweet reward of a sale at the end of your hard work and perseverance.

- **Don't neglect the basics of spelling and grammar.** Your short story might be one of the best out there, but if it's riddled with misspelled words and split infinitives, its other qualities won't matter. Go through your piece with a fine-tooth comb several times before you mail it off to a publisher or editor. If you need assistance with spelling or grammar, pair up with a writing colleague who is strong in those areas.

- **Do allow time for reflection.** Mercurial and restless are your bywords, so your first response to a rejection is often to get the piece back in the mail in the blink of an eye. It's necessary to get your work back out there as soon as you can, but not before you take a hard look at the rejection letter as well as your writing. Slow down, take a deep breath, and force yourself to analyze the response. Before you drop the article into the mail slot again, do you need to make changes? Find them and make them. Doing so could make the difference between a yes and a no the next time around.

· **Don't talk yourself out of resubmitting.** By the time an article or story makes its way back to you, it may have lost some of its luster as far as you're concerned. A piece that has been rejected twenty times might be accepted on try number twenty-one. There might not be anything inherently wrong with your story; the problem could be that you're sending it off to inappropriate markets. Give it another look, and reassess the audience you're targeting.

GIVING and RECEIVING CRITICISM

When you place your work into the hands of a Gemini, be prepared to receive excellent advice not only about how to improve your writing, but how to market your work in interesting and sometimes ingenious ways. Gemini is the zodiac's natural sales and marketing people, and they will go over your manuscript with a discerning eye toward editing as well as selling your product after you've put the finishing touches on the book. Ruled by Mercury, writers born under this sun sign are at once logical in their approach as well as innovative when it comes to subject matter. They rely on their intellect and can sometimes come off as distant or cold, but that's only because their minds are so busy analyzing your work that they forget to infuse the requisite emotion into their comments. Gemini is sometimes accused of being superficial in their approach to things—perhaps even flighty—but the fact is their minds work so fast and furious that by the time most people are at mid-point in thought or action, they have already arrived at the destination. You won't suffer from lack of comments when it comes to a Gemini critique. They will have plenty to say about your work and will be more than eager to share their thoughts with you. Gemini critique partners are eager to assist, but steel yourself against their tendency to fire off suggestions in rapid-fire succession without in-depth consideration of your emotional reaction to the same. It's not that Gemini doesn't care about your feelings—it's a matter of reminding them at times that others react on more than an intellectual level to criticism!

Others might think Geminis, with their intellectual air and adaptable nature, are great at handling criticism, but they would be wrong. Writers born under the influence of Mercury hide a fount of nervousness and sensitivity beneath that devil-may-care attitude and chatty exterior. These writers are eager to receive input on their literary efforts, but take care. Whenever possible, appeal to the cerebral half of their personality when you dole out suggestions for revising their writing. Preface your critique with the positive aspects you noticed in their work, and then gradually move into areas for improvement. Geminis are so changeable at times that they can be maddening. Often, you aren't sure which side of them you might be dealing with on any given day—the open and loquacious Twin or the closed and irritable Twin. Therefore, take cues from their behavior before proceeding further.

TEN PATHS TO PUBLICATION FOR GEMINI

1. **Treat writing like a job.** The fun part of writing is being creative and connecting with others—things you love to do as a Gemini. The not-so-fun part of writing is the actual work that goes along with it. If you are serious about becoming a published writer, you must treat writing as a job and not as a mere hobby. Set a regular schedule for yourself that includes tasks such as researching markets, writing queries, and working on articles. Just as you know what to do when you arrive at your office in the real world every day, you should also know what you need to do on a daily basis to put yourself closer to becoming a published writer.

2. Don't dream it; *be* it. To view yourself as a real writer, act like one. When people ask what you do for a living, don't be afraid to tell them you're a writer. So you're still working at a regular full-time job—that doesn't mean you can't be a writer, too. Explain that you have a double career—accountant (for example) and writer. Get used to seeing yourself as a writer, and don't be shy about identifying yourself as such. It's not uncommon to pick up writing gigs once people find out you're a professional scribe, so advertise your talents!

3. Mind the details. Don't forget to add proper postage on the return SASE (self-addressed, stamped envelope). This seems like a no-brainer to most writers, but the truth is that writers make mistakes all too often. Small details are often forgotten in the heat of the moment. Editors are concerned with obtaining the best content, and they don't have time to baby-sit. Writers are expected to be professionals at the outset, so put your best foot forward on all fronts. Coming up short on return postage brands you as an amateur, and you know you're anything but! If you are mailing to another country, don't guess at the postal process. Ask the local post office for the proper return postage for a manuscript sent outside the country.

4. Sit still! Gemini writers can be like butterflies on caffeine— you're here, there, and everywhere all at once. It may be difficult to train yourself to sit at your desk each day and produce a set number of words or pages, but in the long run, that's the only way to turn your dreams of authorship into reality. If all else fails, purchase an inexpensive egg timer, set it for twenty to thirty minutes, and do nothing but write until the timer rings. Chances are that once you get going, you'll find yourself exceeding your preset minimums and turning out more pages than you ever thought possible.

5. Narrow your choices. The Gemini writer is never without a handful of ideas at any one moment, but you may find yourself wrestling too many ideas at once. When you're unsure of which ideas you should tackle first, nip indecision in the bud by choosing no more than three of your best ideas each week. As the jack-of-all trades in the zodiac, you will be successful in any subject you undertake. The trick for you is determining which subject offers the best potential for a sale and then concentrating your energy on that one area.

6. Conquer one page at a time. *How could I ever complete a 100,000-word book?* you might ask. Given your preference for short, invigorating ventures, writing a book may seem like a daunting task. Break larger projects into bite-size pieces. Instead of scaring yourself with the big picture, realize that books are written by systematically completing small, manageable segments. One page a day for a year will yield a book. A finished chapter a week and you'll have a complete manuscript in a matter of months.

7. Finish it. If you're the typical Gemini writer, you probably have reams of unfinished manuscripts littering your office. It's not that you can't finish them. It's just that the boredom fairy sprinkles her dust on you more often than on many other writer signs. You're blessed with loads of energy, but unfortunately, it's the nervous sort of energy that leads you to drop projects when you lose interest in them. Promise yourself you'll complete one project weekly, whether it's a query letter, poem, or short-short story. As time goes on, you'll pile up stacks of finished pieces for submission. You'll also motivate yourself to take on longer and more extensive writing goals.

8. Get recognized! There are countless writers out there—so what makes you different, dear Gemini? Name recognition, that's what. It doesn't matter if you've published one small article or a thousand articles. If you want to increase your chances of publication, you must get your name out there for all to see. You, of all writer signs, are the perfect marketing person, so print up business cards, build a Web site, conduct a workshop, host an online chat, and do whatever else you can to get your name out there. The more visible and well known you become as a writer, the more chances you have to snag additional assignments.

9. Change your point of view. You're a writer, so you're tempted to look at the publishing game through the eyes of a writer all the time; on occasion, you need to shift perspective and view the landscape from an editor's eyes. Put on your editing hat and take a hard, objective look at your work. If this article came across your desk, what comments would you make to the writer? List the plusses and minuses of the work, then firm up any weak spots before you slip it into an envelope and ship it off to its final destination. Give your submissions one last look—doing so could save you from future disappointment.

10. Jingle it up! Maybe it's not the same as being in print, but having your radio jingle or teaser produced will carry weight on your writing résumé nonetheless. Thousands of radio stations across the country need copy for morning shows and the like, so why not tap into this unique market? Never limit yourself strictly to print and online venues—consider radio and television markets as well.

Exercises for Gemini

Gemini writers are witty intellectuals whose minds work nearly as fast as their mouths do. They are generalists rather than specialists. They take in and process enormous amounts of information in half the time it takes many other people to get with the program. These writing exercises are designed to help those born under the sign of the Twins to strengthen their focus, concentration, and diligence.

1. Describe an object in detail. Choose an object you find interesting—it could be something as simple as a foreign coin, an irregularly shaped rock, or a unique stuffed animal. Take as much time as you need to thoroughly inspect and analyze the object using all your senses. For instance, does the coin have crisp ridges on its side, or have they been rubbed off? What about the rock—does it smell like the ground where you discovered it? And how about the stuffed animal—does it squeak or talk? Grab your pen and paper and write a narrative description of the object using all five of your senses. Take your time and use all your concentration to cover every possible aspect of the object—do *not* rush! The goal of this exercise is to teach you how to quiet your often chaotic mind and focus deeply and for an extended period of time. Use this technique on a regular basis, each time increasing the time you take to observe and write about the object by a minute more until you take no less than a full twenty minutes to compete the task.

2. Write down your dreams. Build a pattern of consistency by keeping a nightly dream journal. While this journal can certainly be used for its idea-generating benefits, the focus here is on daily stick-to-itiveness. Upon awakening, jot down any images or stories you remember from the dreams you had the night before. If you did not have a dream, then record that. Be sure to note your mood and impressions upon awakening, along with any words or images that pop into your mind as you write. Strive to record something each and every morning for at least twenty-one days to get in the habit of recording your thoughts and recollections. This exercise will assist in training your mind to become comfortable with a creative routine.

FAMOUS GEMINI WRITERS

May 22, 1859	Conan Doyle
May 25, 1803	Ralph Waldo Emerson
May 25, 1967	Poppy Z. Brite
May 28, 1908	Ian Fleming
June 3, 1926	Allen Ginsberg
June 8, 1947	Sara Paretsky
June 9, 1956	Patricia Cornwell
June 12, 1929	Anne Frank
June 13, 1865	William Butler Yeats
June 14, 1811	Harriet Beecher Stowe
June 16, 1938	Joyce Carol Oates
June 19, 1856	Elbert Hubbard
June 19, 1947	Salman Rushdie

Writing a novel is like making love, but it's also like having a tooth pulled. Pleasure and pain. Sometimes it's like making love while having a tooth pulled.

—DEAN KOONTZ

Key personality traits: sensitive, intuitive, emotional, purposeful

Symbol: the Crab

Element: water

Ruling planet: the moon

Qualities: negative, feminine, cardinal

JUNE 22–JULY 22

cancer

is the lunar-influenced scribe of the zodiac—emotional, responsive, and perceptive, Centered on home and family, they are individuals who like to nurture others and keep the hearth fires burning. Crabs have an uncanny ability to sense and understand the inner motivations of others, as well as a knack for spotting contradictions between a person's true feelings and his verbal and nonverbal behavior. Respectful of authority and careful to perform any task they are given to the best of their ability, Cancers prefer a comfortable and secure environment. Tradition, family, and history are important to them. Consequently, these moon children may find themselves drawn to subjects that have to do with people's private lives, historical events, and home or family life. Because they are adept at plugging in to the heart and soul of other human beings, they are talented at creating believable characters who are collages of family and friends they know in real life.

Ruled by the moon, Cancer writers are prone to moodiness and withdrawal. In fact, when they feel out of sorts, they can get downright cranky. Empathic and sensitive, moon writers are so in tune with their surroundings and pick up so easily on other people's moods that they shoulder the burden of others' troubles without even realizing they're doing it. The result is total overload, which manifests not only in their physical countenance, but in their mental and emotional demeanors as well. When Cancers get to this point, the protective barrier between them and the outside world goes up in no time flat. They climb into their collective shells like hermit crabs, and won't emerge until they've had a chance to collect their thoughts and recenter. When retreating from the world, Cancers should make the most of the situation by grabbing their journals and recording their thoughts and feelings. The outgrowth of this experience could be stories, articles, or novels.

Four Foolproof Ways Cancer Can Smash Writer's Block

1. Plug in to your past. Family. History. Tradition. These three subjects are close to Cancer's heart. When you're agonizing over what to write next, go back to your beginnings. Make a list of questions about your past, your family's heritage, or the history of your traditions. Did your family celebrate a particular holiday in a different way than the rest of the neighborhood? Did you have a quirky aunt you'd like to know more about? What are some fascinating facts about your heritage? Exploring your past can open doors to article ideas. Keep a list of running questions and refer back to it any time you need a fresh query idea.

2. Flow with feeling. Like your fellow water signs, Scorpio and Pisces, you are awash in intense emotion most if not all of the time. You can't help it; everything has meaning for you, and your moods rise and fall with the moon cycles and the tides. Keep your words flowing in a steady stream by going straight to the source of your being—emotion. Find a notebook and fill it with feelings. Draw columns and label each with a specific emotion. Then write about each particular emotion in detail, taking care to describe in precise terms how each would feel, smell, taste, sound, and look if you took that emotion out, set it on a table, and examined it as an object. Now build a character around that emotion. What would a character personified by surprise look like? Pair your emotion character with others, and explore the interactions between them. Take the exercise further by building scene and sequence around your emotion characters until you have an impromptu story idea you can revise for submission.

3. Borrow a life. Cancer writers have a knack for empathizing with other people. If you can't seem to connect your muse with a story idea of your own, schedule a time to interview a few people you know about their lives. Ask about their childhood and teen years, their likes and dislikes, their philosophy on life, or their family histories. Tell them you are brainstorming ideas for articles, and ask permission to jot down notes from your conversations. (Assure them you'll keep their names and places of residence anonymous if requested.) People love to talk about themselves, and you're more than willing to listen. When you "borrow" other people's lives, you're sure to end up with an abundance of story, article, or book ideas.

4. Keep a diary. The pressure of writing for others under deadline is enough to make you pull your hair out at times. Even more disturbing, creating on command (or on demand) can squeeze the imagination and spontaneity right out of you. On occasion, take a break and reenergize yourself by writing without boundaries in your personal diary or journal. Sit down with no set agenda in mind and allow your thoughts to wander without restraint across the page. Make a date with your muse on a weekly basis, find a quiet place, and seek communion with your inner spark. Every several months, pull out your previous diary entries and relive the creative moment of a particular day or two. Pull five to ten ideas from your writings each month and use them as jumping-off points for articles, stories, or novels.

DEALING WITH REJECTION

Here is a hard truth you may not want to hear, moon-baby scribe: No matter how wonderful your writing may be, there will be someone out there who either won't like it or who won't believe it fills his editorial desires. The truth is a hard thing to swallow, but if you expect to make headway in the world of publishing, this is one truth you'll have to come to accept. The sooner you realize that you cannot please everybody (and that you shouldn't try in the first place), the sooner you'll be one step closer to handling rejection in a more objective and professional manner.

Though your outer shell is as hard as nails and protects you from many barbs in your life, you must work on your soft, inner core in order to mute the sting of rejection. Unlike Leo, who hardly ever questions the excellence of the work he puts out, you have a feeling your work is good at times but not at others. Any attack on your abilities makes a deep wound and ends up stonewalling your progress. Make this your mantra: *Rejection is not personal!* Repeat it daily—or even hourly—if need be. Brand it into your brain by whatever means possible. For you, the best way to counteract the effects of rejection is to stay tough on the outside while cultivating resilience on the inside.

REJECTION DO'S AND DON'TS

• **Do get your feelings out on paper—don't hold them in! Your first reaction to anything negative or hurtful is to hide inside the protective shell you build around yourself.** In the case of handling rejection, this is the last thing you should do, moon child. Instead, grab your journal and jot down all the reactions to having your work rejected—good, bad, and ugly! By purging your pain rather than holding it inside, you face the emotions head-on and clear the path to get back to work right away. Once you are finished, close up your journal and leave the hurtful moment behind once and for all.

• **Don't read more into the rejection than what is actually there.** Cancer is adept at tapping into other people's responses, but all too often you are guilty of imposing your own reactions in certain situations. The end result is a loss of much-needed objectivity. When an editor tells you the short story you submitted was close, but didn't quite meet the publication's needs, that doesn't mean you outright failed. Practice detaching from your purely emotional responses little by little. Get to the point where you can view rejections for what they are—not as you imagine them to be.

• **Do build a network of supportive writing colleagues.** Only other writers can truly empathize with your plight when it's only two months into the new year and you've received six rejections already. Friends and family will sympathize in the wake of yet another no, but a tight circle of writing buddies will know the right words to say and can offer constructive suggestions.

• **Don't keep stacks of rejection letters and torture yourself by reading them over and over.** Cancers are sensitive and prone to living in the past at times, but reliving painful moments when your work didn't make it to publication can only stymie you in the long run. Pasting rejection letters all over the office will motivate some writers, but not a Cancer; rejection slips staring you in the face every single day will only depress you more. Pitch them into the trash!

GIVING AND RECEIVING CRITICISM

Let's face it: Critiques aren't on the top of the welcome list for Cancers. As a water-based, tender-hearted sign, Cancers can be touchy not only when they are on the receiving end of criticism but also when they are on the giving side. They react with deep-seated emotion to everything in their environment, so when they provide an analysis of your work, don't expect superficial comments or suggestions. They will delve into your writing as well as into what they feel may be the motivation behind your words. Expect detailed comments and questions scribbled in the margins of your manuscript. They will care about your answers to these

questions, so don't consider their queries rhetorical. Above all, never dismiss their suggestions or comments unless you care to make your Cancer friends feel grumpy, unappreciated, and very put out. Even if you don't plan to implement their advice, express your heartfelt gratitude and thank them for their comprehensive assessment of your work. Like their water-based cousins, Pisces and Scorpio, they will give you in-depth commentary that will elucidate and illuminate.

As the recipients of criticism, Cancers give off an air of thick-skinned detachment, but don't let the outside covering fool you. They are masters of pseudoprotection, but the reality is that if you prick them with the wrong comment, they will fixate on it and counter with resentment. It's not that Cancers can't or won't take criticism; it's more a matter of presentation. One must temper one's words when offering suggestions to the moon child. Like the tides that shift under the lunar influence, Cancer's moods shift from moment to moment. Even worse, you may not always be able to get an immediate read on how your Cancer friends are feeling. Crabs are masters at retreating into their shell or throwing up barriers. When they're injured—either mentally or emotionally—it will be a long time before they will let you get close to them in that way again. The bottom line is this: It's okay to deliver an honest opinion on the Cancer writer's work if you take care to temper it with a huge dose of tact.

10 Paths to Publication For Cancer

1. **Write every day.** Come rain or shine, good day or bad, you'll need to put your pen to paper every single day to keep yourself in a smooth rhythm, Cancer. Emotions can sometimes send you running for the hills, ready to pull that armored shell over

yourself to keep out the world. Resist the urge to withdraw when you're having a less-than-perfect day. Instead, journal about your feelings, and then, once you gain some distance from the moment, use what you've written as the foundation for your work.

2. Make friends with the past. Remember all those family photo albums and scrapbooks you have? What about all those genealogy notes you have tucked away in your closet? Now's the time to drag them out, sort through them, and evaluate them as possible writing projects. Every life has a story, and given the Cancer's penchant for the past, you're just the person to write about it. Using your stash of photos and notes, make a list of ten potential articles, then query Web sites and print publications that focus on history or genealogy.

3. Go on a writing retreat. Look in almost any writing publication's classifieds and you're apt to discover at least one advertisement offering a writing retreat up in the mountains or near a beach. Take time away from the everyday grind of life and spirit your muse away to a writing retreat at least once a year. You'll surround yourself with like-minded souls and pick up handy tips and advice for advancing your writing career.

4. Search for the new. Keep an eye open for listings of publications just starting up. They'll be in search of content (and possibly staffers), and now is the time to show them what you're all about. It won't hurt to send them a query along with a sample of your work and your writing résumé. This type of initiative can help you get your foot in the door and may snag you a regular writing gig.

5. Go back in time. With your love of history and the past, publications focusing on historical people and events are a draw

for you. Draft a list of five to ten intriguing historical events or people. Brainstorm at least two article or story ideas for each item on the list. Then consult your market resources and isolate publications that center on history and use freelancers for content. Query them.

6. Get crafty. Whether you're into crocheting, woodworking, scrapbooking, quilting, or the lapidary arts, there is a whole host of publishers specializing in craft magazines and books. Cancers are nurturing and known for their crafting skills (especially skills for enhancing their homes), so if you're one of these crafty moon children, why not capitalize on your artistry? Any craft key word will yield countless returns from a premier Internet search engine. Most craft publishers have a presence of some sort on the Web. Bookmark the guideline pages in a specific folder and set forth on your quest to nail down an assignment.

7. Mothers, unite. If you're a Cancer mother, various lists, message boards, and organizations exist to cater to your special needs. With many women staying at home to raise children and build their writing careers at the same time, you'll be in good company and receive the specific support and encouragement you'll need. Scope out lists on well-known hosts such as Yahoo! Groups (groups.yahoo.com), Google Groups (groups.google.com), and Topica (lists.topica.com), and type in *writing moms* to search for the latest listings.

8. Try something new. It's all fine and good to settle into a comfortable routine, but your love of the security and safety of the predictable is no reason to keep your writing life in the same old groove. Success may be waiting for you just around the corner, but if you never turn the corner, how will you know? Promise yourself you'll delve into a new genre or type of writing each month for a whole year. Do research and find out what options are out there for you, then select the ones that most appeal to you. Set a goal to submit at least one different piece of writing—different for *you*, that is—by the end of each month.

9. Open yourself up. Essays are a hot commodity in hundreds of consumer magazines across the globe. They're also the perfect way to examine the inner workings of your mind and your soul while connecting with readers (and, consequently, publishers). Unfortunately, Cancer doesn't volunteer to bare his soul unless it's absolutely necessary. Teach yourself to open up more and share with your readership by forcing yourself to look at the good, bad, and ugly of your life. It's a scary step, but by putting your personal experiences in writing and offering the lessons you've learned for public consumption, you could collect new acceptances and clips to add to your résumé.

10. Cash in with celebration tips. Holidays are the perfect time for friend and family gatherings—something you dearly love—but it's also the perfect time of the year for specialty articles. Do you have the best recipe for Christmas cookies on the planet? Know how to perfectly seduce your partner for Valentine's Day? Then sell your tips and tricks for holiday revelry to consumer publications. In general, most magazines need eight months or more of lead time for holiday-themed articles, so begin querying your article ideas a year in advance.

Exercises for Cancer

As the natural empaths of the world, Cancers can best connect with their readers by using their writing to nurture and instruct others on many levels. Emphasize the positive aspects of your sensitive nature and connect them with your creativity through the writing exercises below.

1. Take notes. Carry a small notebook with you wherever you go. Go to a mall, a beach, or a library—anywhere you can observe people. Pick one or two subjects and observe them from a comfortable distance. Note their clothing, gestures, and facial expressions. Imagine what each person is like: name, profession, habits, personality, fears, and dreams. Sketch a character profile of each person and elaborate with as much detail as you can get on one or two pages. Keep your word sketches in this notebook and then use them later for inspiration when you begin selecting characters for your next work of fiction.

2. Interview an object. Imagine four inanimate objects, each one with a different degree of hardness, softness, flexibility, and fragility. Examples might be a rock, a feather, rubber, and glass. List these items on a piece of paper, then begin at the top of the list and concentrate on each object for no more than a minute. Write about this object and its qualities for no less than five minutes, detailing what each object is and what it would tell you about itself if you were to interview it. For instance, if you spent your days as a feather, what might your life be like? Delve into how a feather might view the rest of the world and what emotions it might experience in the process.

cancer

FAMOUS CANCER WRITERS

June 22, 1906	Anne Morrow Lindbergh
June 22, 1964	Dan Brown
June 24, 1950	Mercedes Lackey
June 25, 1903	George Orwell
June 26, 1915	Norman Cousins
July 4, 1927	Neil Simon
July 8, 1953	Anna Quindlen
July 9, 1945	Dean Koontz
July 12, 1817	Henry David Thoreau
July 21, 1899	Ernest Hemingway
July 22, 1936	Tom Robbins

Don't think. Thinking is the enemy of creativity. It's self-conscious and anything self-conscious is lousy. You cannot try to do things. You simply must do things.

—RAY BRADBURY

Key personality traits: assertive, bold, confident, demonstrative

Symbol: the Lion

Element: fire

Ruling planet: the sun

Qualities: positive, masculine, fixed

JULY 23–AUGUST 22

Leo writers are the consummate entertainers of the zodiac. Leos are born with a flair for the dramatic, so a Leo's writing will never be described as boring or dull. They are generous with their talent and will pull out all the stops to dazzle their readers with whirlwind plots and larger-than-life characters. Leos who specialize in nonfiction writing have a special knack for making even the most prosaic of subjects fascinating to their audience. When put center stage, no one performs with more brilliance and moxie than a Leo. You can bet a Leo author's book signing or workshop appearance will be dynamic and filled with high-octane energy that sizzles and crackles through the entire crowd. Leos love the spotlight, and they're great at commanding everyone else's attention. If you need a quick course in Publicity 101, find the closest professional Leo writer and be prepared to take notes on how to do it right!

Conversely, while Leos are blessed with more verve in their little fingers than the rest of us can ever hope to possess, the downside is that they are also prone to bouts of intense assertiveness and occasional egocentrism that reaches beyond the pale. Less-than-kind reviews easily prick Leo's self-esteem. A Leo's charge is to rise above the fuss and remain the regal and outgoing writer she is—even if she must grin and bear it. Leos have to strive to maintain an even temper in the face of critics and reviewers who are not as complimentary about their work as they expect them to be. Although Leos usually don't find themselves depressed over negative comments about their work like a sensitive Pisces might, they are more apt to become indignant over the slight. Leos want to win over everyone with their appealing prose and sparkling personality, and find it hard to acknowledge that they will not always succeed. (Some people just don't know talent, do they?)

Four Foolproof Ways Leo Can Smash Writer's Block

1. Organize your thoughts. You were born with the golden touch of organization—so put it to good use! Don't let fuzzy thinking trip you up when are poised on the verge of a literary breakthrough. Set up a file folder system on your computer to track ideas from brainstorming sessions as well as information from market listings. Once a week, scan through your idea list and match ideas with your market listings.

2. Control your emotions. The more you try to write, the fewer words come out of your fingertips. You sit for hours on end, staring at a blank screen, fiddling with paperclips, and chewing on pens or pencils. Sound familiar? Writer's block is a catch-22 situation: The more you worry about it, the worse it gets. Leos are action-oriented individuals who want to stay in motion, so writer's block is torture for you. However, the more emotion you generate through frustration, the more you are likely to struggle.

3. Eliminate obsession. Leo fully expects to succeed in every endeavor undertaken. If you're stalled on a particular idea, you won't let go until you make it work—somehow, some way. The truth is, not all ideas and approaches to certain subjects work. Abandoning an ineffective approach doesn't equal failure; it indicates wisdom on your part. Toss aside all the woulds and shoulds you have regarding writing and forge new paths. If one idea isn't bearing fruit for you at this time, push it aside in order to make way for fresh material. Wasted time—and energy—does little more than halt your creative progress.

4. Remember to ruminate. Realize that writing involves an ebb and flow of activity and rest, and both are needed in order to produce the best material. Get familiar with and find comfort in the active and passive phases of the writing life. I like to call these phases the productive phase and the rumination phase. Both have their merits and both have their place. As in the concept of *wu wei* (or "nondoing") in Taoism, there is an appropriate rhythm and time for every action. This doesn't mean you should never take action at all; rather, you should go with the flow, a notion that will seem foreign to most Leos. Often, you develop writer's block when you approach your writing in a forceful manner. More often than not, a forceful approach results in frustration and anger, but no tangible results. Give yourself permission to contemplate before you generate.

DEALING WITH REJECTION

You don't let rejection get you down in the dumps, Leo. You counter rejection by working that much harder to show everyone else that you *can* and *will* succeed. Proud and strong willed, you may feel a tidal wave of emotion over having your work passed over, but you will never let anyone else know how much rejection stings if you can help it. You might dismiss the pain with a laugh or wry smile while puffing up your regal Leonine exterior, as is customary for you, but deep inside, the cut will smart. You won't believe you aren't good enough; to the contrary, most of the time you'll see your work as exemplary and wonder why the editor, agent, or publisher didn't recognize your sheer talent. While some may see this attitude as pompous or conceited, the truth is that this attitude may protect you from deeper hurt in the long run. While Cancer and Pisces often find themselves wounded to the core, you come out swinging and ready to prove your worth. For you, it's all about pride.

Though you feel rejection as much as any other writer sign, you are prone to lash outward rather than examine inward. Instead of turning your emotions toward other people in a whirlwind of indignation, learn to sit with the less-than-happy news and be honest with yourself about your abilities and efforts. No one is perfect, not even you; as much as you dislike seeing yourself in a critical light, there are times when your ego must take a backseat to the work. When you examine your writing for weaknesses and listen without prejudice to comments received from editors about your writing, you will become more honest and open with yourself. Learn to accept rejection not as a slight, but as a gift that will help enhance your talent.

Rejection do's and dont's

- **Do consider that while your idea may be workable, your angle or approach may be off.** Your vision of an article or feature may not match up with the editor's vision of your subject matter. Be open to making the requisite changes to slant the piece according to editorial objectives. Remain flexible, and exhibit genuine enthusiasm for alterations to your piece.

- **Don't dismiss a publication just because it has rejected your submissions once, twice, or even countless times.** Leos have a conquer-all attitude, and that makes you both tenacious and the perfect go-getter. If you aren't quite hitting the mark with a publication, maybe it's time to get out a stack of current issues and study the recent content. Compare your latest rejected piece to those accepted in the magazine, making a list of your work's hits and misses. Rework or start over again, if necessary. Likewise, if your book proposals aren't generating enough positive interest, delve into the publisher's current releases and jot down common themes and subject matter. Use those as a jumping-off point for your next book pitch.

• **Do harness that natural Leo assertiveness and bounce back from rejection right away.** Don't let more than a day pass before you submit another query or piece of work while you are revamping the rejected piece for another submission round. Keep your writing in circulation. Track your queries and submissions through a computer database you've developed yourself or through writers' software you've purchased.

• **Don't let your ego prevent you from listening to—and taking—advice.** Leo writers are a confident and competent lot, but that doesn't mean you can't find room for improvement. Check your ego at the door when you need to and listen without prejudice to advice given by your editor, agent, or critique partner. Constructive criticism from others will give you an objective view of your work, and while you may not always agree with the verdict, every writer at one time or another must swallow her pride in order to inch closer to publication and payment.

GIVING and RECEIVING CRITICISM

Leos are the best. If you don't believe that, just ask them! While this might be an overstatement (but not by much), the fact is that Leos are born performers who take extreme pride in everything they do. Not only are they the best at what they do, they also have fine insight into what does and does not work for other writers. Leos are generous with praise for others and genuinely want to help out fellow writers. Warm and outgoing, the Lion will take you aside and brashly outline all the positives and negatives of your manuscript. Leo is as generous in doling out praise as she is in dishing out criticism. Be careful to listen to what the Lion tells you, however, for she believes the time she spends assisting you is worthwhile. Leos expect appreciation for their efforts. Treat the nuggets of advice they give you like pure gold (because they are!) and don't forget to lavish Leos with sincere thanks.

In the same vein, balance is the key when critiquing a Leo's written work. Focus on the positive aspects of the writing, not just the parts that need improvement. If you cannot say anything good about a Leo's writing, then it is probably best not to open your mouth at all. Pride is a huge component of the Lion's personality, and she responds best when you recognize her substantial contribution. While she will appreciate your constructive comments, tread with care and consideration. Deliver critical commentary in as positive a light as possible. If you point out a problem, it would be wise to provide a fitting solution for repairing it. Leos are interested in actions and solutions instead of open-ended complaints that aren't clearly explained. In order for them to respect you, more often than not you'll be required to prove your legitimacy as a writer yourself. After all, if you expect the Lion to take your advice, you'd better be worthy of her time and attention.

10 PATHS TO PUBLICATION FOR LEO

1. Bite your tongue! Even if you believe an editor or an agent is wrong in rejecting a piece of your writing, resist the urge to confront her about what you perceive to be a mistake on her part. Although you may have an inborn talent for writing, Leo, you must also accept that you don't have all the answers and that you won't be able to dazzle every single person the first time out.

2. If you've got it, flaunt it. Most Leos are born with charisma, so put it to good use by making a list of your talents and experience, then pitching surefire ideas based on your list. Love to skydive? Born to bungee jump? Find markets that match your passions, and query away.

3. Court the locals. What better place to start than in your own backyard? Dozens of writing opportunities abound in your city and state, and Leo's just the type to fit the bill. Does your city paper need a part-time stringer to cover local events? Does that new company up the street need someone to put together brochures or the monthly employee newsletter? You're never shy about asking and you're unafraid to risk a no, so why not turn on that Leo charm and land an assignment or two while you're at it?

4. Take the road less traveled. There are countless writing venues to explore. Leos love excitement and the potential for new and uncharted territory. With your natural exuberance and schmoozing abilities, you can wend your way into the trendiest parties and most exclusive hotspots with the world's movers and shakers. Pursue uncommon writing gigs, such as gossip columns, society pages, and political punditry.

5. Network, network, network! Go to as many writing conferences, workshops, and writers' club meetings as you can fit into your busy schedule. With your stunning Leo personality, you're sure to make a splash and cultivate business and industry connections. You'll get the heads-up on the newest paying markets, most recent editorial post changes, and latest job openings for freelancers.

6. Turn on the ambition. Idealistic and bold, you're known for going straight to the heart of the matter. Seek out markets beyond the standard listings in books and on Web sites. Focus on an area you want to specialize in and search for professional or organizational Web sites that are connected to your preferred area of expertise. If you aren't sure a company or organization uses freelance writers, offer your services in a professional letter outlining your experience.

7. Organize, plan, and manage. Leos are close to flawless in their ability to organize and execute a successful plan of action. Kick your talents into gear by developing a personal system for logging potential writing markets, tracking queries, monitoring submissions, and gauging your daily productivity. Getting published hinges on a writer's ability to follow an effective strategy toward specific goals.

8. Mind your clips. Editors often ask for samples of your work to get a feel for your writing style and your voice. Showcase your abilities by maintaining a portfolio of your work; when asked for clips, put your proverbial best foot forward. Leos are adept at wowing an audience, so pull out all the stops and show 'em what you can do!

9. Percentages count. Each year, Writer's Digest Books publishes a new edition of *Writer's Market*, a huge compendium of market listings that covers book publishers, consumer magazines, and trade publications—just to name a few. Most publications report what percentage of their content is written by freelance writers. Scour *Writer's Market* and list markets in your preferred genre that get 60 percent or more of their material from freelancers. Hit those markets first with queries or submissions. The higher the percentage of freelance content, the higher the publication should be ranked on your must-query list. By using this strategy, you'll increase your chances of snagging a go-ahead for your articles and stories.

10. Start small. While it would be nice to land your first article in *GQ* or the *Atlantic*, chances are you won't. Don't overlook smaller publications—so-called *littles*—in favor of the larger, glossier magazines. While competition is fierce no matter which publication you target, if you're just starting out in the business, you'll have a better shot at landing an acceptance from a publication amenable to novice or intermediate writers than from a larger market that predominantly uses established writers.

Exercises for Leo

Ambitious and confident with a dash of generosity, Leo writers sparkle like gems in the literary world. Because you live large, you seek bold ways of asserting yourself as a writer. Large or complicated projects are never daunting for you, and your approach is positive and courageous every single time. You are in charge of your life on all fronts and you are turned on by power and prestige. Others may see your assertiveness as an overabundance of pride, but you see it as accentuating your assets. Get connected with your bold inner spirit through writing exercises designed to focus on your particular astrological assets.

1. Consider the legacy you want to leave as a writer. In your mind's eye, see your career—beginning now—and write out the highs and lows of your writing life, culminating in your greatest achievement. Now imagine it's twenty years from now and you're being fêted by the greatest scribes in the industry. What would you want them to say about you as a person and as a writer? If you believe that what you dream can become reality, then might you be able to create your career successes from this point forward? Draft a vision for your future sales, acceptances, and accomplishments. Be as detailed as you can be, citing the exact minimum number of articles, poems, screenplays, or novels you intend to produce each year. Script your upcoming accomplishments, whether they include winning a Hugo or making the bestseller lists—then, little by little, transform your written plan into reality.

2. Be a celebrity. You are perfect for center stage, Leo. You love the glare of the spotlight and you are the consummate entertainer. Select a favorite celebrity or noted author and imagine stepping into her shoes for twenty-four hours. Who will you select as your subject, and why? What must it be like to spend a day at J.K. Rowling's desk or in Stephen King's office? Write an essay titled "A Day in the Life of …" and detail every (imagined) aspect of your celebrity's life, from the breakfast she eats in the morning to her specific writing routines. Prefer movies to manuscripts? Travel into the star-studded world of Johnny Depp or Julia Roberts and conjure up a treatise on how he or she spends the average day.

FAMOUS LEO WRITERS

July 24, 1895	Robert Graves
July 24, 1802	Alexandre Dumas, *père*
July 26, 1856	George Bernard Shaw
July 26, 1894	Aldous Huxley
July 27, 1824	Alexandre Dumas, *fils*
July 29, 1972	Wil Wheaton
July 30, 1818	Emily Brontë
July 31, 1965	J.K. Rowling
August 1, 1819	Herman Melville
August 4, 1792	Percy Bysshe Shelley
August 5, 1850	Guy de Maupassant
August 6, 1809	Alfred, Lord Tennyson
August 11, 1921	Alex Haley
August 15, 1885	Edna Ferber
August 19, 1902	Ogden Nash
August 22, 1920	Ray Bradbury

When asked, "How do you write?" I invariably answer, "one word at a time."

—STEPHEN KING

Key personality traits: critical, precise, methodical, diligent

Symbol: the Virgin

Element: earth

Ruling planet: Mercury

Qualities: negative, feminine, mutable

AUGUST 23– SEPTEMBER 22

Virgo

—meticulous is your middle name. Practical scribes born under the sign of the Virgin approach writing in an orderly and precise manner—for them, nothing less will do. If they are required to research for an article, they will dig deep to locate sources and information, leaving no stone unturned in the process. They are analytical to the extreme and are never satisfied with a mere surface treatment of anything, and most certainly not in their work! Virgos don't shirk their duties when it comes to answering the call of the muse. In the end, they deliver sparkling and intelligent prose and poetry second to none. Reliable and deadline conscious, Virgos are diligent in completing writing assignments on time.

Sound like an editor's dream? Not so fast!

On the flip side, if Virgo writers aren't careful, they may fall prey to bouts of overzealous perfectionism. It isn't uncommon for a Virgo writer to complete numerous revisions before he drops a manuscript into the mailbox. Even then, he will obsess over whether his writing will make the grade—Virgos are easily their own worst critics. Razor-sharp exactness is an admirable trait, but Virgos must balance their perfectionist tendencies with the realization that absolute perfection isn't always attainable.

Four Foolproof Ways Virgo Can Smash Writer's Block

1. Write first, analyze second. Virgos are sticklers for accuracy when it comes to putting pen to paper. While striving for excellence has its merits, overemphasis on perfection can block even the savviest of writers. Shove the ever-present internal critic aside in the beginning, get your thoughts down on paper, and then go back and clean up the mess.

2. Don't always begin at the beginning. As a Virgo, you're inclined to move through orderly steps to reach any goal, believing that the shortest path from A to B is a straight line. However, when it comes to writing, starting at the beginning can be daunting—especially when you're staring at a blank sheet of paper! Break out of your methodical mode by dropping your characters into the middle or the end of a story and then writing your way back to the beginning.

3. Build your characters first, your plots second. Perhaps you already know your story's ultimate destination, but you're unsure how to get there. Such uncertainty often blocks Virgo scribes for days or weeks on end. Forge a different path by honing your characters' traits—physical, mental, and emotional. Character motivation is what drives a story, so train your Virgo focus on constructing your characters first—deciphering their motivation—and then allow the plotline to flow from their actions.

4. Dig up new angles using the four W's and one H. Journalists know the quickest way to get to the meat of a story is to ask who, what, where, when, why, and how. Whether you're writing nonfiction, fiction, or even poetry, by applying these probing questions to your writing project, you'll not only dredge up fresh ideas, you'll satisfy the natural detective in you as well.

DEALING WITH REJECTION

Rejection happens, dear Virgo! No matter how thorough, conscientious, and hard working you are, there will be days when even your best efforts will yield little more than a *Thanks, but no thanks* form letter from an editor or agent. You have a natural tendency to be hard on yourself, so it's important to gain a healthy perspective on rejection. Consider the process as a necessary means to improving your skills and advancing your abilities. Writing is a discipline that requires time and experience to master; allow yourself the necessary time to grow and develop. Coming into your own never happens overnight!

Perfectionism is a double-edged sword for Virgo writers. On one hand, your tendency toward precise detail is an admirable quality for a writer. On the other hand, when perfectionism is magnified to the extreme, the result is lack of confidence and a reticence to continue submitting work. The agony you find yourself in is often of your own making. You may not be able to control the response to your work, but you can control your reactions to rejection. The word *rejection* doesn't equal failure. Furthermore, past rejections do not dictate future realities—or acceptances!

REJECTION DO'S and DON'TS

· **Do begin reworking your query or article immediately.** Scope out an alternative market, then resubmit your piece within a short period of time. Resist the urge to pore over your work to the point of obsession; get it back out there in circulation! Perfectionist as you are, those articles and stories will never satisfy you 100 percent. Do your level best, then let go.

· **Don't emphasize the negatives of the situation.** Instead, seek out the valuable lessons you've learned from the rejection and translate that knowledge into tangible improvements in your writing. Repetition, it's been said, is the mother of skill. There's an unspoken equation in a writer's life: The more you try, the greater your chance of success. Don't give up too early in the game.

· **Do realize there are levels of rejection, and you can glean clues from each.** For instance, a handwritten editor's note offering specific comments about why your piece was rejected is more valuable than a generic form letter. The more personal the rejection, the more it is an indication that your writing was close, but not on-target enough for acceptance. When you start receiving fewer form rejections and more personal ones, you know you're on the right track!

- **Don't let your emotions put you into a rut.** Virgo writers harbor deep feelings and they can easily become discouraged. Use the emotions you experience from your rejections to spur you to work that much harder on your next submission. Be proactive rather than reactive. Turn that negative into a positive, driving force.

GIVING AND RECEIVING CRITICISM

As the consummate analysts of the zodiac, Virgos are in their element when asked to assess a piece of writing. They will easily point out errors others may have missed, and have no problem isolating problem areas in grammar, syntax, and punctuation. While the symbol of Virgo is the Virgin, the modern-day symbol for the Virgo writer might as well be the red editing pencil. Virgos won't offer surface comments or fluffed-up praise for the sake of stroking another's ego. When critiquing others' writing, Virgo writers should remember to present their matter-of-fact, logical comments in a reader-friendly way. Work as hard picking out the positive aspects of the manuscript as you do noting the negative points. Refrain from offering criticism without following up with specific tips for improving the troublesome areas. Above all, strive to deliver an assessment of your subject's writing that is more constructive than critical.

As receivers of criticism, Virgos aren't welcoming. Though they are usually harder on themselves than anyone else is, they conceal a streak of apprehensiveness that is magnified by others' judgments. Virgos prefer to deal with the concrete rather than the abstract, so when appraising a Virgo's writing, provide concrete approaches to bettering the work. Just as Virgos should strive to temper their comments with compassion, it's even more important for critique partners to offer praise to Virgos when they deserve it.

10 PATHS TO PUBLICATION FOR VIRGO

1. Submit, submit, submit! When your aim is to send out a certain number of queries per week, set a concrete goal and stick to that number. Always keep your work in circulation.

2. Explore new genres and markets. Break out of your preconceived notions of what you can and cannot write. You may discover new skills and talents you've never tapped before. Once a nonfiction writer doesn't mean never be a fiction writer.

3. Read as much as—if not more than—you write. Vary your reading material by sampling from all categories of writing, from nonfiction to fiction and poetry. Steamy romance novels differ from mysteries in flavor, but rules of plot and characterization apply equally to both genres.

4. Examine current bestsellers. Detailed by nature, Virgos will welcome the chance to analyze various tomes to seek out the methods bestselling authors employ to hook readers and keep them coming back for more.

5. Mind your markets. Whether you're aiming to sell a short story or pitch an article, keep up on the latest market information. Purchase the current version of *Writer's Market*, and scour the Internet for other sites that list viable markets for writers.

6. Build a support group. Writing can be a lonely endeavor, and solitude can grate on a Virgo's nerves. Find or build a group of writing buddies who will offset your sign's natural tendency toward pessimism with optimism and encouragement.

7. Set goals. Virgos are born organizers, so take full advantage of this attribute. Develop a system for tracking your writing goals, and map your progress on a weekly and monthly basis. Use submission-tracker programs, calendars, and reminder prompts to keep yourself focused.

8. Establish contacts. Virgos are reserved to the core, and aren't known as the outgoing social butterflies of the zodiac. Networking in the publishing business will open up a new world of information and advice from both novice and veteran writers alike.

9. Diversify. Commercial businesses and nonprofit organizations also have writing needs—from brochures to press releases and newsletters. Publicize your writing services through advertisements, business cards, and cold calls. Build a portfolio and use it to target other publication venues.

10. Promote yourself. Modest as you are, Virgo, in order to win at the publishing game, you must promote yourself. Awareness and name recognition can go a long way toward getting your foot in the door.

Exercises for Virgo

Virgos appreciate exactness, and you can be sure any plot they develop will be constructed in a tight and precise way, with no loose ends. To connect with the essence of the Virgo writer within, give these writing exercises a whirl.

1. Outline your project. Details are the specialty of most Virgos, so put your natural talent into play by developing an outline for your latest article, short story, or book. Grab a stack of index cards and use them to map out character traits and list important plot points for your novel. Tack up the index cards on a bulletin board in flowchart order so you can visualize the narrative flow of your manuscript. If you are writing a nonfiction article, use the cards to keep track of quotes and other information you plan to introduce or discuss in the beginning, middle, and end sections of your piece.

2. Relax with freewriting. Regimentation can be helpful for writers in many cases (especially when it comes to deadlines), but Virgos need to relax and let their muse out to play every now and then—without restrictions! Find a regular block of time each day to write without any rules or restrictions. Use a timer (a gadget that is sure to please your sign) and set a limit of twenty to thirty minutes.

FAMOUS VIRGO WRITERS

August 24, 1951	Orson Scott Card
August 27, 1871	Theodore Dreiser
August 28, 1749	Johann Wolfgang von Goethe
August 30, 1797	Mary Shelley
August 31, 1908	William Saroyan
September 1, 1875	Edgar Rice Burroughs
September 4, 1920	Craig Claiborne
September 7, 1887	Edith Sitwell
September 11, 1862	O. Henry
September 11, 1885	D.H. Lawrence
September 12, 1880	H.L. Mencken
September 13, 1916	Roald Dahl
September 15, 1789	James Fenimore Cooper
September 15, 1890	Agatha Christie
September 21, 1866	H.G. Wells
September 21, 1947	Stephen King

People who cease to believe in God or goodness altogether still believe in the devil. I don't know why. No, I do indeed know why. Evil is always possible. And goodness is eternally difficult.

—ANNE RICE

Key personality traits: balanced, sensuous, aesthetic, diplomatic

Symbol: the Scales

Element: air

Ruling planet: Venus

Qualities: positive, masculine, cardinal

SEPTEMBER 23–
OCTOBER 22

LIBra is all about balance. It is no accident that Libra's symbol is the only inanimate object of the zodiac (all others are represented by animals or humans), and it's no wonder Libras have the ability to detach themselves from situations and render level-headed assessments. Unpredictable ups and downs and chaotic atmospheres set Libras on edge. They prefer orderly, harmonious, and aesthetically pleasing surroundings. One of their gifts is the ability to look at the world and the people around them with impartiality and diplomacy. Mediators at heart, they can always see both sides of a situation. Libras are born under the influence of the planet Venus, and so have an artistic bent. They may not only write, but paint or sketch as well. Romance and relationships are two of their greatest concerns, and one of their main goals is to avoid conflict with others. They would rather compromise with an editor about their work than cause discord or disagreement. Hence, they will work well with most higher-ups in the publishing industry when it comes to getting down to business. Libras respect authority figures (regardless of whether they agree with them) and, in turn, are usually respected for their professionalism.

Often described as easygoing and laid back, Libra writers can slip into the habit of being a bit too relaxed in their dealings at times. In addition, they can be so caught up in seeing both sides of an issue that they become stuck in limbo and reluctant to make a firm decision. As the consummate team players, Libras work well with others and are excellent collaborators on writing projects. They are genuine moderates who have the gift of objectivity; Libras make excellent editors because they can look at a piece of work with an unbiased, fair point of view. Most Libras are even-tempered and they are drawn to a variety of artistic endeavors—especially writing. They are versatile scribes who have the ability to write across genres and styles.

Four Foolproof Ways Libra Can Smash Writer's Block

1. Press on. When the going gets tough and ugly, the first instinct for a Libra is to sit back and relax. Those words will come to you eventually, right? Don't bet on it. Writing can get down and dirty at times. Your muse can play a mean game of hide-and-seek—only you might be inclined to disappear into other pleasures instead of tackling the block head-on. Don't give in to your instincts. Press forward with renewed enthusiasm for your project.

2. Do it in longhand. Libras are touched by Venus, a planet associated with the arts and creativity. Get back to the basics of writing by using paper and pen instead of firing up your word processor or computer. For an interesting interlude with your muse, treat yourself to the luxury of parchment paper and a finely sharpened feather quill dipped in homemade ink. The act of hand-forming letters and words will often stimulate your creativity.

3. Pick up where you left off. Getting started can be the hardest part of the writing day. When finishing your writing for the day, leave a hook to help yourself get started in the morning. Dialogue is an excellent starter tool, so instead of concluding your writing day at the tail end of a conversation, intentionally leave off in the middle of a verbal volley between characters. When you pick up your pen again, you'll slip back into the rhythm of conversation in no time at all. If you're writing nonfiction, stop at a crucial point in the article.

4. Compose writing prompts. When it comes to staving off writer's block, advance preparation is the key. Open a folder in your computer or divide off a section of your journal for writing prompts. Put five to ten writing prompts in your notes for starters, then add more each week for when your creative well runs dry in the future. Write the prompts yourself, if possible. Prompts ask open-ended questions or present ideas worth further exploration. They can be a word, phrase, or sentence that you feel compelled to continue with your writing. An example might be: *Terry and Joe approached the notorious haunted house of Pinewood Grove. As they tiptoed closer to the dilapidated old mansion, they suddenly noticed …* Pick up the story from there and run with it.

dealing with rejection

You are known as one of the people pleasers of the zodiac, dear Libra. You want to like others and be liked by others in return. So when rejection rears its horrendous head, you may have a hard time dealing with it—whether it's your first rejection or your hundredth. When you turn in an assignment, you want it to please everyone on all levels—starting with others first. You are extreme in your quest to please others before you please yourself, so making the grade with your editor, agent, and readers is primary for you. To you, a rejection notice means failure to please. And that, dear Libra, is a hard thing for you to accept.

Just as perfectionism is a sticking point for your astrological neighbor Virgo, your sticking point is realizing you can't please everyone all the time. The only way to combat this is to work on accepting this fact and shifting your concentration to doing the best work you can. Worrying about how everyone will perceive you is a waste of time and energy. It can sap you of inspiration and trap you into nonaction—another danger for Libra writers. Focus on your craft, do the best job you can, and the rest will fall into place.

rejection do's and don'ts

• **Do trust the process.** The writer's journey is one of ups and downs in which surprises (both good and bad) abound. Libra writers prefer a level playing field in their lives, but the writer's journey is rife with potholes and detours. Take the letdowns in stride, revel in the glories along the way, and have faith in the process. With perseverance and confidence, you'll rise above any obstacles in your path.

- **Don't hesitate to act.** One of Libra's weaknesses is getting caught in a pattern of indecision because you're not sure how best to react. When you receive a rejection, don't be indecisive about which course of action to take in response. Should you rewrite the article? Is the article fine, but the market wrong? Which response is appropriate in this case? These questions can mire Libra writers in procrastination purgatory. Don't let yourself slip into this habit. Instead, make a pact with yourself to take decisive action within no more than forty-eight hours of a rejection.

- **Do focus on the present.** It's all too easy to fixate on past refusals and to lose sight of present opportunities. Keep your vision trained on what you can do today to advance your writing career, and avoid dwelling on past disappointments. Each time you garner a rejection, counter it with a proactive activity geared toward making new progress.

- **Don't be shy.** If an editor returns your manuscript with notations you don't understand, don't hesitate to send a brief letter politely asking for clarification. If you intend to pitch another piece to that same editor in the near future, it's to your benefit to ask for clarification. The more information and advice you comprehend, the better your chances are of selling future articles or stories to the publication.

GIVING AND RECEIVING CRITICISM

Fair and balanced is the battle cry of genuine Libras, so expect nothing less when a native born under the Scales critiques a piece of writing. Libras want to be honest and aboveboard in all their actions, but they don't like to ruffle anyone's feathers in the process. They will give your work an eagle-eyed treatment couched in language that is both helpful and discreet. Socially adept, Libras realize it's more to their advantage to keep writing friends and mentors than to make enemies, even if inadvertently. They will never set out to trample another writer's ego, because they wouldn't want the same done to them. Libra writers do not revel in swiping at others when he or she is giving criticism on others' work. A pure Libra spirit will put forth nothing less than cultured and humane advice on writing and will steer clear of crass and overly snippy editing behavior!

Libra writers should remember it's okay to mention a problem with a manuscript if they see it. Other writers want to know how they can improve their work, so follow your sign's mantra for balance in all things by mentioning both positive and not-so-positive points in your analyses. You won't do the recipient any favors by glossing over an apparent problem in her work. By conveying the truth in an unvarnished, yet professional way, you'll earn the respect of the person receiving the critique.

The best way to deliver criticism to Libras is with decency and good manners. Libra writers hate anything coarse or lacking decorum, so approach them with measured responses. Appreciation of their ideas is another must when dealing with Libras, so be sure to emphasize the positive when critiquing their work (especially if you've included quite a few comments on less-than-praiseworthy aspects of their writing). When they're on the receiving end, Libras should remain open to ideas from others and reserve judgment (there are the Scales again) until they've heard the whole story.

10 PATHS TO PUBLICATION FOR LIBRA

1. Review your options. As the most impartial writer sign of the zodiac, you are the perfect candidate to pen reviews for everything from books to computer applications. Contact small publications and Web sites to inquire if they use freelancers for reviews. If so, write for them to build your credits and credibility as a reviewer. As you gain experience and clips, expand to larger markets for more pay.

2. Get "tipsy." Magazines and online sites are always looking for short, informative articles that provide lists of tips of interest to their readers. Tip sheets and bulleted lists on topics ranging from organizing a home office to keeping kids busy after school are popular with publications of all types. Take inventory of your everyday knowledge and use it to pitch short, educational pieces to print and online venues.

3. Play around! If you're interested in writing for stage or screen performances, begin at the local level. Most cities and towns have at least one community theater or similar organization. Get involved in the theater community, either with acting or set decoration (you'd excel at either, by the way). Learn the ropes, study play format, then approach the theater's director about trying your hand at writing a play for the local actors to perform.

4. Write from the heart. One of the best ways to get published is to target subjects that resonate with your values and beliefs. Libras are concerned with equality and fair treatment, so mull over ideas for articles you can contribute to consumer advocacy markets. Contact local organizations, set up meetings, then offer freelance writing and editing services to them.

5. Practice the art of doing it now. Contracts and assignments won't magically appear—you have to take action toward specific goals in order to snag them. Are you waiting for your kids to start school? Putting off writing until you can afford a better computer? There are a million excuses for not writing, but none of them hold water. If you want to write, you must make it a priority, starting today. Every day, finish at least one task—however small—geared toward increasing your chances of publication.

6. Combine your talents. Do you paint or draw as well as write? Writing either picture books or higher-level chapter books for children could be a viable route to publication for you. Subscribe to newsletters and seek out organizations that cater to children's writers, such as Write4Kids.com (www.write4kids.com), the Society of Children's Book Writers & Illustrators (www.scbwi.org), and the Canadian Society of Children's Authors, Illustrators, and Performers (www.canscaip.org), among many others.

7. Use your sense of style. Interior decoration and design are two areas that appeal to most Venus-influenced Libras. Take advantage of the abundance of decorating and design publications on the stands by querying them with creative ideas for sprucing up work and living spaces.

8. Make writing a habit. Writers who submit often are writers who get published sooner and more frequently. In order to submit often, you must make writing a daily habit, just like brushing your teeth. Talent does not equal automatic publication; neither does persistence and determination, but you'll get a lot further toward your goals with the latter. Talking about writing is one thing, but doing it is the only sure way to produce tangible results.

9. Educate yourself. Not sure what to put in a book proposal or how to craft a query letter? Unsure what a SASE is? Boost your chances of publication by participating in writing workshops, taking classes, and attending writers' conferences.

10. Do it yourself. For many writers, self-publishing is a serious option. Author M.J. Rose turned to self-publishing when traditional publishers wouldn't publish her work. Her book, *Lip Service*, was originally self-published. The book was eventually picked up by Atria/Pocket Books and became a hit that catapulted Rose into the role of successful author and mentor to countless writers. However, self-publishing can be risky and is difficult at best. To decide if self-publishing is a route worthy of your consideration, visit the Get Published section of WritersDigest.com (www.writersdigest.com/topics/getpublished.asp) for more information.

Exercises for Libra

Libra writers are motivated by values such as fairness, justice, and equality. They also have a profound respect for beauty, whether it's manifested physically, mentally, or spiritually. They are social butterflies who yearn to connect with others. Hook up with your muse and give her a workout with these exercises devised with Libra traits in mind.

1. Find beauty in an everyday object. Nobody does a better job of discovering hidden beauty than Libra. You instinctively know what's tasteful and cultured. Now it's time to take a different tack with beauty—or your perception of it. Find an everyday object that you and others would usually describe as anything other than beautiful. How about a withering plant? Is there an old, bald tire out in your garage? After you've selected your item, find a quiet place (perhaps outside on the porch or inside at a work table) and fully examine the item. Make a note of the basic appearance of the object, noting any irregularities or worn spots. Once you've described the basic attributes of the item, shift your mind and set out to find the inherent beauty of the object, however ugly or rough you might think it is at first glance. Again, beauty is in the eye of the beholder. Use your imagination and writing skills to unearth the hidden charm of the object. Write about your discovery.

2. Find your strength in op-ed pieces. Diplomacy is your strong suit, Libra. Scan the newspaper or listen to the news, then select from the news one current event or issue of an explosive or sensitive nature. Practice your op-ed skills by drafting an article either supporting or opposing the issue or topic you chose. If you aren't sure of all the angles of the issue, research as required, then write the article as if you planned to submit it for publication. Once you're finished, find at least one market you can actually submit to, and do it!

FAMOUS LIBRA WRITERS

September 24, 1896	F. Scott Fitzgerald
September 25, 1897	William Faulkner
September 26, 1888	T.S. Eliot
September 30, 1924	Truman Capote
October 3, 1900	Thomas Wolfe
October 3, 1925	Gore Vidal
October 4, 1941	Anne Rice
October 10, 1924	James Clavell
October 14, 1888	Katherine Mansfield
October 14, 1894	E.E. Cummings
October 15, 1917	Arthur Schlesinger Jr.
October 15, 1844	Friedrich Nietzsche
October 16, 1854	Oscar Wilde
October 16, 1888	Eugene O'Neill
October 17, 1915	Arthur Miller
October 19, 1931	John le Carré
October 21, 1929	Ursula K. Le Guin

Firstly, there is no such person as Death. Second, Death's this tall guy with a bone face, like a skeletal monk, with a scythe and an hourglass and a big white horse and a penchant for playing chess with Scandinavians. Third, he doesn't exist either.

—NEIL GAIMAN

Key personality traits: intense, compelling, secretive, determined

Symbol: the Scorpion or Eagle

Element: water

Ruling planet: Pluto

Qualities: negative, feminine, fixed

OCTOBER 23–
NOVEMBER 21

SCORPIO

writers are enigmatic and rarely in-decisive, and approach their craft with an intensity that is both admirable and awe inspiring. The writers of this sun sign are not only dependable, they are coura-geous and confident. They can exhibit as much steadfastness as their Capricorn siblings, but they also have a deep and wide vein of fearlessness. An air of certainty pervades every project Scorpio writers undertake. When they tell you they will complete a book manuscript or sell their screenplay, you can take that to the bank—and cash it in. Scorpios know how to work people and are often hypnotic and charismatic. They can influence deals in their favor and get colleagues to do exactly what they want in most cases.

Passion and confidence make for an impressive and unstop-pable writer. On the other hand, those two elements, if not kept in check, can leave a bad taste in other people's mouths. Scorpios work at such an intense level that most people cannot even hope to keep up with them. Forceful and demanding, Scorpios size up situations and those involved at lightning speed, and make final decisions in record time. The term *waffling* has never been used to describe a Scorpio personality. People who cross the Scorpion writer may be forgiven, but the slight will never be forgotten. The bottom line is this: If a Scorpio truly wants to become a profes-sional writer, no one and nothing on this earth can or will stop him. However, Scorpios must be careful not to leave broken souls and singed egos in their wake!

FOUR FOOLPROOF WAYS SCORPIO CAN SMASH WRITER'S BLOCK

1. **Write from the senses.** When it comes to connecting with the senses, no other writer sign can hold a candle to you, dear Scor-pio. The easiest and fastest way for you to beat writer's block is

to escape the world's chaos and reacquaint yourself with every aspect of your senses. The touch of a piece of fabric can evoke strong memories; the smell of a flower can bring back a flood of feelings from years ago; the sight of an animal in a natural habitat may bring forth a poem you never knew you had inside. Explore all your senses, then write about the experience.

2. Give up control. Most Scorpios loathe feeling out of control in either their personal or professional lives. Maintaining a rigid mindset can often have an adverse effect on your creative spirit. Remember Scorpio, this world won't stop spinning nor will your life crash around you if you step back and allow your muse to take control (without direction from your logical mind, that is). New ideas cannot be developed in such a stringent way. Trying to fit your muse into a pre-planned scheme is like herding cats—it's impossible! Chill out and let your mind play every once in a while. Unsupervised, of course!

3. Allow your characters to grow. Are you ever smack dab in the middle of a story when suddenly you're not sure where your main characters will go next? Although you have an idea of who your characters are in the beginning of a story, chances are they will say and do things you aren't expecting. To avoid getting stuck in your fiction, allow your characters to grow and change in accordance with the path of the story—even if that path isn't one you originally intended to follow.

4. Develop an idea portfolio. Visual stimuli are an important part of most Scorpio lives, so why not create an idea portfolio filled with pictures meant to kick your muse into gear? Grab a camera (type and cost don't matter) and spend part of a day out and about shooting scenery, people, and things. Bring a notebook with you and take notes about your subject matter: where you were, what time you took the shot, and any other pertinent details. It's been said a picture is worth a thousand words. Now that you've taken a bevy of photographs of a variety of subjects, look at them through a writer's eyes and find the thousand words (or ideas) captured in each of them.

DEALING WITH REJECTION

Unlike your water cousins, Pisces and Cancer, you won't sit in the corner and lick your wounds for long when rejection comes knocking at the door. The old saying *I don't get mad—I get even* applies to you. Scorpions are competitive, willful, and unrelenting once they've made the decision to become a published writer. It's okay to be driven and forceful in your crusade to gain recognition for your work, but avoid turning the process into an us-versus-them competition. As you've read numerous times before here and elsewhere, rejection isn't about you. It's about whether the publication has a need for what you've written. If you've delivered a piece that matches a publication's tone and style, and covered a topic not overdone within their pages, you may get a chance to see your work in print. If, for any of a thousand other reasons, your article or story doesn't make the grade, that isn't necessarily a reflection on your worth as a writer or human being.

Because of your intense temperament, you're apt to slip into anger rather than sadness. Neither emotion is a healthy means of coping with rejection. If not kept in check, the groundswell of emotion will ultimately surface in your dealings with editors and agents—and not in pleasant ways. Release pent-up frustration in your personal journal after you've received a rejection. Be as pitiless, brutal, and vicious as you like in your private responses. Allow yourself time to cool down from your rant, then embark on a new approach to your work. Ignoring your emotional reactions to rejection is never healthy, but giving your rants and complaints free rein isn't a smart thing to do, either—unless you employ clandestine means.

Rejection Do's and Don'ts

- **Do keep your stinger in check.** Scorpio writers are forceful individuals who frequently refuse to take no for an answer. As a result, rejection of their work might trigger a harsh word or two. Learn to accept the inescapable fact of rejection, and practice responding in a measured and controlled way. Lashing out won't win you any points with editors.

- **Don't get too personal.** You have a way of latching on to people and getting under their skin—in either a good or a bad way. While you may want to work your intense personality magic on those at the higher levels of the publishing world, your usual modus operandi may backfire on you. Keep your correspondence crisp and professional at all times, and avoid engaging in conversation that veers off into personal areas.

- **Do fantasize on occasion.** No matter what you do, sometimes you can't seem to get past the sharp pangs of rejection. When all else fails, engage your imagination to make yourself feel better—if only for a short while. Did your editor get stuck in rush-hour traffic that morning for hours? Did he wake up on the wrong side of the bed for a whole week? Whatever ludicrous scenario you develop in your head, use it to shift your outlook from annoyed to amused. As the fictional character Mary Poppins once commented, "A spoonful of sugar helps the medicine go down." Concoct your own mental medicine to cope with rejection.

- **Don't forget your checklist.** Different publishers have different requirements for submissions. Some prefer synopses and sample chapters, while others want an outline of each chapter plus additional specialty items, such as a short explanation of why you wrote this particular manuscript. Make sure you don't forget anything when you prepare your package for mailing. Compose a checklist and tick off each item as you add it to the envelope. This way you can be sure you don't leave anything out—one less reason for a publisher to reject you out of hand.

GIVING and RECEIVING CRITICISM

Scorpio writers can be either your best writing colleague or your worst critic. If you are looking for an honest critique of your work in progress, the Scorpio writer will deliver a precise assessment of both your strengths and weaknesses. However, don't expect their critiques to be superficial and fluffy. They won't boost your ego just to make you feel better about yourself. Instead, you'll receive an accurate, in-depth review that highlights their almost uncanny ability to separate the wheat from the chaff—and then some. Scorpios often possess a sixth sense about people and situations, so they may uncover hidden motivations of your characters (and even yourself!). Scorpio writers have an innate sense of what drives human beings. That talent alone serves as a plus when it comes to writing on a myriad of levels and in a variety of genres.

Diplomacy is the name of the game when offering a critique of a Scorpio's writing. It's not that they don't appreciate your input about their work, because they do value sincere and constructive criticism. However, the Scorpio writer demands two things from any would-be critic: expertise and tact. If you're not as seasoned a writer as the Scorpio is, then chances are your comments will be dismissed out of hand. Scorpios are serious about their writing, and they require an equal amount of care from those with whom they share their words. To avoid the sting of those born under this sign, approach the task with confidence, but avoid talking down to them. Remaining in control is important to them, and they won't put up with any other sign that tries to make them feel small, inferior, or insignificant. If you dare rankle a Scorpio by trashing his writing (either intentionally or unintentionally), then do so at your own peril.

TEN PATHS TO PUBLICATION FOR SCORPIO

1. **Confess your sins.** Scorpios have sensuality to spare, so why not capitalize on your erotic tendencies. Confession magazines are not a thing of the past; in fact, there are plenty looking for tell-all stories to whet their readers' appetite for scandal. Whether you write based on fact or fiction, you can spin yarns of deceit and betrayal for cold, hard cash.

2. **Explore your dark side.** Writers born under the sign of the Scorpion love the darker side of life, with all its bizarre and twisted facets. Ruled by Pluto, Scorpios are drawn to the hidden and unseen, and so are attracted to the shadier side of human beings. Horror, suspense, and thrillers are attractive to you, so capitalize on your penchant for the macabre. For links and markets, visit sources such as the Horror Writers Association (www.horror.org) and International Thriller Writers (www.thrillerwriters.org).

3. **Plumb the depths of the soul.** You're a water sign, so nothing that happens in life is superficial to you. You feel every single ounce of life experience deep down to the core of your being. As such, you may find writing opportunities in publications such as *Psychology Today*, which examines human behavior and the motivations behind it.

4. **Engage in supernatural "writes."** The occult and paranormal are strong draws for any Scorpio writer. The realm of the unexplained—from poltergeists to exorcisms to teleportation—can provide fertile ground for your writing and help you find a place with both small and large book publishers. Contact local ghost hunters in your area and ask if they will let you tag along on one of their investigations, then pitch the story to local and national markets—with photos!

5. Get down and dirty. Sex sells, and who better to sell it to hot-blooded readers than yourself, dear Scorpio? Erotic and even porn markets are worthy of consideration for most Scorpio writers. Those who prefer to keep the sizzle under wraps and the language to PG may contemplate penning a sweeter variety of soft erotica. Of all writer signs, none is better suited to deliver wild and wicked prose than you—the one noted in astrological circles as a master of the boudoir!

6. Thrill your readers. With your ability to delve into the psyche of others, mysteries and true crime may be attractive for you. If you're new to writing mystery, legal suspense, or crime, join a professional writing organization that specializes in these genres, such as Sisters in Crime (www.sistersincrime.org), Mystery Writers of America (www.mysterywriters.org), or the North American branch of the International Association of Crime Writers (www.crimewritersna.org), among others.

7. Tap into transformation. There are countless ways to reinvent oneself and change one's life, and Scorpio can be a wonderful author of articles and books on self-transformation. You have a knack for bringing to light hidden facets of the human psyche; delve deeper and find ways sto share your discoveries.

8. Seek out the unusual. If anyone's willing to veer off the beaten, tried-and-true path, it's the Scorpio writer. You're not afraid to venture into uncharted territory or taste strange fruit. Given your fascination with the unusual and weird, your writing may find a home in publications that cater to fans of body piercing, tattooing, or other body modification. Other signs may cringe and shy away from these markets (and toss away a chance to make sales); capitalize on other writers' refusals to touch such unique subjects.

9. Use your connections. Know an old high school friend who works for the city newspaper? Does a former sorority sister work as an intern for a large magazine in the Big Apple? Scour your list of family, friends, acquaintances, and friends of friends to seek out possible contacts in the publishing industry. Often, contacts made through people you know can help you get your foot—and words—in the door.

10. Take a shot. Even if you're not an expert at photography, maybe it's time you honed your picture-taking skills. Many publications pay more for articles that are accompanied by quality photos. Check guidelines carefully and submit photographs according to requirements. Offering your photographs in addition to your articles can increase your chances of making more sales.

Exercises for Scorpio

Scorpio writers are intense and focused people who excel at plumbing the depths and secrets of the human condition. More often than not, mystery, sex, and intrigue are particular areas of interest to them. Use the writing exercises below to slake that thirst.

1. Create a compelling character from a name. Pick a name, any name—preferably, one you would select for a character in your newest as-yet-unwritten tale (you pick the genre). Write up a combination character sketch/psychological profile of this character, making sure it is as in-depth as it can possibly be. Delve into your character's childhood, defense mechanisms, phobias, and fatal flaws. Once you have completed your detailed sketch, build an intense, ground-shaking story around your character.

2. Profile someone fascinating. Jot down who you consider to be the five most intriguing or sought-after newsmakers of today. Your potential subjects can be local celebrities, national personalities, or major movers and shakers from any segment of society. Your main concern is to select someone who fascinates you. If you had the chance to interview (or pen a profile on) each of these people, what questions would you ask—and why? What roads would you take to lead your readers into the secret realm of these people, and how would you write about them in the most creative, yet informative, way? Note your reactions and methods next to each person's listing. Peruse your list, and then select one subject for an article or interview. Now ferret out a market suitable for your proposed article or interview. Craft a professional, well-researched pitch and submit it to an editor right away!

FAMOUS SCORPIO WRITERS

October 23, 1942	Michael Crichton
October 25, 1941	Anne Tyler
October 27, 1914	Dylan Thomas
October 27, 1932	Sylvia Plath
November 1, 1871	Stephen Crane
November 2, 1942	Shere Hite
November 7, 1913	Albert Camus
November 8, 1900	Margaret Mitchell
November 10, 1960	Neil Gaiman
November 11, 1821	Fyodor Dostoevsky
November 11, 1922	Kurt Vonnegut
November 13, 1850	Robert Louis Stevenson
November 18, 1939	Margaret Atwood
November 21, 1694	Voltaire

A classic: something that everybody wants to have read and nobody wants to read.

—MARK TWAIN

Key personality traits: blunt, jovial, optimistic, intellectual

Symbol: the Centaur or Archer

Element: fire

Ruling planet: Jupiter

Qualities: positive, masculine, mutable

NOVEMBER 22– DECEMBER 21

Sagittarius

is the gregarious, blunt, and freedom-loving philosopher of the zodiac. Subjects such as law, religion, and politics fascinate these jovial Jupiter-influenced writers—but that's just for starters! The cultural dynamic of the global community will appeal to these writers, but they won't want to be tied down to exploring just one side of their creative personality. They are usually ravenous readers and are willing to write about nearly any topic. That's because they explore every aspect of their world and possess an inquisitive nature.

Sagittarius writers are great conversationalists, and this comes through even on paper. They make the reader feel comfortable—almost as if the reader is sitting across from them, having a fireside chat. Sagittarius fiction writers are attuned to the characteristic ebb-and-flow of dialogue, and know where to place pauses for emphasis. They love stories full of suspense and intrigue. Travel may also be a prominent part of their fiction writing, as Sagittarians are no strangers to wanderlust.

Four Foolproof Ways Sagittarius can Smash Writer's Block

1. **Go beyond the ordinary.** You are fascinated by people, cultures, and the extraordinary. You love to seek out the strange and intriguing elements of the world, so translate your fascination into unique ways of viewing your writing. Depart from mundane subjects, and brainstorm ten to twenty questions you have about the mysteries of the world around you. If you were a reader, what fresh topics in philosophy, anthropology, and religion might pique your interest? Jot those down and freewrite on each, one by one. Choose a handful of promising starts and find markets for them.

2. Take a trip. Sagittarians can abide only so much of the same old thing, whether it's surroundings or people. The travel bug lives in your psyche and you will nourish it as often as you're able. Use those occasional jaunts to the next city, state, or country to dig up ideas for new stories or articles. Set aside a travel log for capturing the impressions of your journeys and recording the sights, sounds, and smells of new places. When you return home, pick out one particular characteristic of your trip—such as the sound of jazz in the streets of New Orleans—and pinpoint ways you can transform that memory into a concrete, salable pitch. Don't stop at articles, however. Travel guide publishers are always on the lookout for fresh views on vacation spots or quirky getaways, so keep one finger on your maps and another in *Writer's Market* for possible book ideas.

3. Break through the barrier. Inertia can block even the mentally active Sagittarius. Even if you think nothing is destined to flow from your fingertips, type or move your pen in spite of your pessimism. Ten minutes of effort is usually enough to break the invisible barrier of inertia and get you back to writing. *What will I write?* you may ask. It matters not what you put on the paper in the beginning, only that you put something down—whether it's a word, phrase, or expression of any kind. The act of forming words and sentences (even if they have no meaning) gets the process started, and in most cases you will find a thread of thought you can weave into a workable idea in no time flat.

4. Get familiar with your surroundings. Thousands of ideas—and opportunities to break open your creativity—are around you right now. You might not really see them, however. Close your eyes for a few minutes, then open them while pretending you're seeing the world through fresh eyes. What's on your desk? A plant? Paperweight? Picture frame? What do you see about these ordinary objects that you can morph into an exaggerated description or story? When was the first paperweight produced, and who was the inventor? What is the native land of your desk plant, and how was the plant first discovered? Use an extraordinary view of ordinary objects to propel you through your creative block.

DEALING WITH REJECTION

Many an astrologer has commented on the Sagittarian's favorable relationship with Lady Luck, a direct result of the influence of Jupiter. The Sagittarius writer takes rejection of his work in stride because he has an optimistic streak a mile wide. Or ten miles wide, to be more accurate. While some Archers swear they aren't competitive, deep down they are just as driven as their fiery cousins, Aries and Leo. The difference is they aren't as overt or boisterous in comparison. They hit their marks by careful aim. Each rejection makes them more determined to scale that big mountain of editorial slips in front of them and turn those negatives into positives. While other writer signs sulk, pout, and curse at steady refusals, the Archer views rebuffs as a challenge.

While you react better to rejection than most other writer signs, you *are* affected by it. But while disappointment at rejection is outwardly apparent with other writer signs, either you put on a poker face and pretend it doesn't bother you, or you laugh it off—until you get home, that is. Then you'll pull the burrs off your heart and vow vengeance. What you need to cultivate most is humility and objectivity. Yes, your writing may have few flaws, but it will never be perfect. There's always room for improvement, and it won't hurt for you to self-administer a strong dose of reality on occasion.

Rejection Do's and Don'ts

· **Do keep your sharp Sagittarius tongue in check.** Bluntness is the hallmark of the Centaur, but when you are dealing with editors, agents, and publishers, it is better to bite your tongue than to slip up and ruin your chances of working with a publisher or publication ever again. Accept constructive criticism with grace, follow the suggestions given, and resubmit.

· **Don't challenge authority.** Rebellious at heart, you might be tempted to submit a piece that is far different from the regular features in the publication you're targeting. Don't do it! While you may think your offbeat charm will win over the editor, the truth is that it will brand you as a novice who refuses to follow the guidelines. Wait until you have an established relationship with an editor before you fully exert your individuality.

· **Do be honest with yourself.** Although they are noted for bluntness with others, Sagittarians aren't always as candid with themselves. Take off those famous rose-colored glasses you wear and try on some bifocals—you may need to take a closer look at the errors you keep making in your queries or proposals. It may hurt a bit, but in the long run you can only benefit from being as brutal with yourself as you are with others.

· **Don't be a pain.** Because Sagittarians are restless by nature, a week can seem like a year to you. Once you submit a piece for consideration, don't hound the publication for a response. Fire signs are go-getters poised for action, but in the publishing world, those who have tact and patience are rewarded. Most editors prefer writers who are easygoing and patient with the process. Don't overshadow your work with a disagreeable, impatient attitude that could result in a no instead of a yes.

GIVING and RECEIVING CRITICISM

Like their symbol, the Archer, Sagittarius writers are straight shooters—sometimes too straight and on the mark. When it comes to critiquing, they will never intentionally pump up others with heaps of false praise. However, they do tend to exaggerate on occasion, although they may not realize it. If your writing is lacking, Sagittarians will flat-out tell you what the problems are instead of stroking your ego. However, minutes after they shoot you down with blunt comments and pointed remarks (when your self-esteem is about to crash into the ground), they'll realize they were too harsh and try to salve the damage they've done. Usually this entails a lot of backtracking, as in *The characters were boring and dull,* but *I think they are diamonds in the rough, and by the time you work on them, they'll sparkle!* or *The dialogue is contrived; but I'm not that great at dialogue myself, so don't listen to me!* (followed by a nervous laugh). Later, when recipients of their criticism are smarting from their razor-sharp, poison-tipped arrows of truth, the Archer will shrug and ask *What did I do? Didn't they want an* honest *critique?* The trouble with Sagittarians is that they deliver straightforward responses, but these responses are rarely tempered with tact. If you keep this in mind when dealing with the Sagittarian writer, then you'll save yourself a lot of grief!

Sagittarians take comments and advice to heart, but when they walk away they will incorporate only what works for them, because they always strive to remain true to their own vision. So feel free to lay on the constructive criticism to your heart's content with Sagittarius—even if you cut him a bit, the wound will heal in record time. Sagittarians are optimists to a fault, so even if you tell them their work sucks, you won't deter them from reaching their goals. They like to think big and act big, so if you tell them their short story doesn't quite cut it for publication, they'll do one better and begin plotting an entire novel. They are restless and always seeking to expand their vision in new ways. The best strategy with an Archer is to give suggestions in an open-ended way that allows them freedom to expand on your advice. *This won't work* is closed and restrictive. To earn the respect of a Sagittarius, you'll need to revise to *This won't work; however, if you flesh out the middle of the tale with backstory, it's salvageable.* Before you close down one path, always give directions for a promising detour.

10 Paths to Publication for Sagittarius

1. Go global. Domestic markets aren't the only avenues to publication, dear Sagittarius. With your love of culture and affinity for picking up different languages—and chances are, you already speak at least one other foreign language, if only at a novice level—international markets are an avenue you should explore. Ferret out both print and online venues as targets for your article pitches, and locate mailing lists and Web sites that cater to writers for international publications.

2. Get in touch with your inner animal. Represented by the half-human, half-horse Centaur, Sagittarians have an abundant love of animals, especially horses. Parlay your fondness for all two- and four-footed creatures into opportunities for publication and pay by scoping out magazines and book publishers who specialize in one of the multitude of creatures that populate this earth. Don't stick to the obvious cat or dog coverage; investigate the diverse offerings of how-to books and magazines on such exotic and unexpected creatures as Chinese water dragons, Indonesian Savu pythons, and African Grey parrots.

3. Grab your notebook and go. Sagittarians love to travel, whether the trip's fifty miles down the road to a local chili cook-off or five thousand miles away to an island in a faraway ocean. Travel writing was invented for the Archer, and you're the perfect correspondent for trekking all around the globe and sending in stories that capture the essence of newfound terrain. One scan of travel publications through online databases or a print market book, and you'll discover countless opportunities to earn a check by combining your love of writing and travel.

4. Become found in translation. If you are an expert in speaking one or more foreign languages, consider translation work as a means of publication. A quick trip through any major online book outlet will yield thousands of results of foreign works that have been translated into English by writers and scholars. Profit from your lingual expertise by translating written work originally set in a foreign language into your native tongue.

5. Ponder for payment. Archers are known as the unmatched philosophers of the zodiac. There's nothing you like better than to analyze and pontificate on an array of philosophical subjects. From ontology to epistemology and from Aristotle to Voltaire, you Sagittarians are sure to find a veritable laundry list of subjects to write about.

6. Sport your stuff! Rare is a Sagittarian writer who doesn't have a fondness for at least one type of sport—either watching it or (preferably) participating in it. Take a stroll through the birthdates of well-known athletes, and you'll discover a fair share of Archers in the mix. Whether you're an active bystander or a rabid team player, writing about sports personalities, teams (both local and national), and players is one route you should consider for getting your words into print.

7. Syndicate your sagacity. Is there a limit to your willingness to dole out wisdom and judgment on a staggering number of topics? In a word, no. Ruled by Jupiter, your mind is expansive and inquisitive, which makes you a generalist at heart. There's hardly a subject you're not familiar with, or haven't done some cursory research on. Your far-reaching wisdom will invariably show up in columns and editorials, because you love to express your view to anyone who will listen. Work on highlighting your expertise and knowledge, then pitch ideas for regular columns and features, either in your local paper, a regional magazine, or online. Once you've made a name for yourself, expand your reach to include national publications, with the ultimate goal of syndication.

8. Delve into the divine. Sagittarians are attracted not only to philosophy, but to religion (or the lack thereof). Whether you're an atheist or an evangelist, the odds are high you have strong opinions on all things theological. Regardless of your spiritual bent or lifestyle, there are a host of publications and book publishers out there in search of writers who can communicate with readers on the subject of religion in a thoughtful and erudite manner. Consult your print or online market resources for further information on current markets.

9. Give your pen a workout. Physical fitness goes hand in hand with an active or sporty lifestyle, so it only stands to reason that Archers are interested in keeping themselves fit. Known for taking a holistic approach to their health, Sagittarius writers are concerned not only with the physical, but with the mental as well. Focus on your particular area of fitness interest, and research consumer publications that deal with fitness, health, and wellness. Don't forget to look into body-shaping and weight-lifting magazines as well.

10. **Write what you don't know.** Some writer signs should write what they know. For you, Sagittarius writers, the instructions differ. When you're just starting out, it may be best to stick with the familiar, but at some point you'll need to expand and to test your limits. You don't have to be an expert in anything to write about it. I know; as a Sagittarian myself, I've published articles on everything from thoracic surgeons to doulas (and I've never worked in any of the career fields I've written about). Bone up on the necessary research, and query the finest experts available for killer quotes and information. Explore beyond the normal boundaries and you'll increase your chances of landing more assignments.

Exercises for Sagittarius

Sagittarius writers have an innate curiosity about their world and the people who live in it. These exercises will assist you, dear Sagittarius, with unearthing your inborn affinity for places, people, and cultures as a whole. Although Sagittarius writers are usually fearless in the way they plunge into writing, even the most daring Sagittarians will occasionally fall into the abyss known as writer's block. Therefore, treat writer's block like a scorned, possessive lover who is hell-bent on forcing you not to write by beating you over the head with unwanted (and unwarranted) criticism of your work. Sagittarius writers are idealists at heart; it's time for that loud-mouthed stick-in-the-mud to shut his trap so you can skip along your merry way to writing without boundaries—imaginary or otherwise.

1. **Go on a musical journey.** Visit your local library's audio section or search the Internet for legal downloads of global or world-beat music. Select one or two collections, or build your own playlist of songs that introduce you to the instruments,

beats, and rhythms of music from a country that is largely unfamiliar to you. Settle yourself in a quiet environment, and spend at least thirty to sixty minutes listening to the music. Close your eyes and let images wander through your mind. Note how the music alters your mood. After your listening session, engage in at least fifteen minutes of freewriting. Record the thoughts and images that flashed through your mind while you were listening to the foreign music—do you see characters, events, and story lines developing from your session? Consider the possibilities for how you can parlay those notes into a workable outline for a short story or even a book about that country or culture and the people who live in it. Evaluate the options for research, and begin your writing journey in earnest.

2. Go on a mythological journey. Delve into the ancient mythologies of a civilization that intrigues you. Study the religious and philosophical stances of that civilization, and then narrow your emphasis to one aspect. Consider the approaches you might take to this aspect of the ancient civilization, and then seek out markets that cater to informative features on historical, religious, or philosophical views.

FAMOUS SAGITTARIUS WRITERS

November 22, 1819	George Eliot
November 22, 1869	André Gide
November 27, 1937	Gail Sheehy
November 28, 1907	Alberto Moravia
November 29, 1832	Louisa May Alcott
November 29, 1898	C.S. Lewis
November 30, 1835	Mark Twain
December 2, 1948	Elizabeth Berg
December 5, 1934	Joan Didion
December 11, 1918	Aleksandr Solzhenitsyn
December 14, 1503	Nostradamus
December 16, 1775	Jane Austen
December 16, 1917	Arthur C. Clarke
December 17, 1903	Erskine Caldwell
December 17, 1929	William Safire

The only real advice you can give anyone is to keep writing. Eventually, hopefully, you'll be published in a small literary journal and can work your way up from there. I don't think pushiness helps at all. It's unbecoming and bespeaks a talent for self-promotion rather than for writing.

—DAVID SEDARIS

Key personality traits: responsible, proficient, organized, persistent

Symbol: the Mountain Goat

Element: earth

Ruling planet: Saturn

Qualities: negative, feminine, cardinal

December 22– January 19

Capricorn

Capricorn has the ambition and discipline to make it to the pinnacle of success. Capricorns are steady, reliable, and undeterrable when it comes to keeping the eye on the prize. They will keep moving toward the finish line long after most writers have veered off course from discouragement or frustration—and there's no doubt they will reach it. Plodding along at a smooth and determined pace, Capricorns are the epitome of the hard worker. Never lacking the ambition and wherewithal to complete any task, they are born knowing that it takes extended effort (and sometimes sacrifice) to get where you're going. With a stripe of leadership a mile wide, they exude quiet confidence and remarkable resilience. They never doubt that they'll come out on top if they just keep their focus on the end results—especially if those results involve financial compensation. Capricorns never work without some incentive; they're all about status and monetary benefits. Some may call the Goat greedy, but the truth is that they're honest about wanting appreciable recognition for their efforts. There's nothing wrong with that, is there?

Admirable as the faultless Capricorn work ethic is, the shadow side of Capricorn is a tendency toward impatience with others, sprinkled with a dash of occasional arrogance. While it's true they have much to brag about, Capricorns must keep in mind that, while others might not be as structured and dutiful as they are, they do possess qualities that make up for it. Work styles vary from person to person; Capricorns must develop patience and acknowledge that it's all right when collaborators do things a bit differently. There are many ways to tackle an assignment, and while one method works for the Goat, it may not fit the modus operandi of anyone else.

Four Foolproof Ways Capricorn Can Smash Writer's Block

1. Don't over-research. Research is admirable and often essential in order for you to produce your best work, but don't use it as an excuse to put off writing if you find yourself facing a block. If the words aren't flowing, you might convince yourself that you are contributing to the work by engaging in research. In such cases, you *are* contributing to the work, but at the expense of the writing itself. While it's okay to take a short detour if you trip over a specific detail that requires expert verification, don't use research as a get-out-of-writing-free card if the going gets tough. Camping out at the library is no substitute for actual productivity.

2. Break out of the rut. Stable and resolute as you are, you tend to stick with what makes you comfortable. This might inadvertently cause a stubborn case of writer's block on occasion. The tried and true might seem like a safe bet to the Goat, who thrives on certainty and direction, but by staying in a predictable pattern you may inadvertently end up stifling your creativity. Change isn't always a bad thing. Everything in life involves some sort of risk—even writing. Take evasive action against writer's block by forcing yourself away from ingrained patterns every now and then.

3. Manage stress. You're all about hard work and discipline. When other writer signs have reached their limit and are eager to throw in the towel, you are just getting started on your long and (sometimes) arduous literary journey. To maintain steady forward motion and avoid pitfalls, keep a tight rein on stress in your life. Capricorns are noted for appearing to keep their cool under pressure. While it may seem they're in control on the outside, they're often just shy of the boiling point inside. Stress is the one stumbling block you're most likely to come across, so prepare for it ahead of time by starting and sticking to a regimen of your own choosing to keep unnecessary upsets at bay. This regimen could include adding positive writing affirmations posted throughout your home office or joining a writers group for support and encouragement when the going gets rough.

4. Recapture your original motivation. Power and status mean a great deal to Capricorns, who work hard and expect to be paid handsomely for their efforts. While there's nothing wrong with focusing on financial rewards, it's important to remember that writing should be more than just a means to an end. Chances are you didn't start writing with the sole goal of making money. You probably began the journey with the intention of showcasing your talent and informing others. All work and no play makes a dull Capricorn, so strive to recapture all the reasons why you became a writer in the first place. When you're fixated on finances to the extreme, it's easy to short-circuit the creative spirit and sabotage yourself.

DEALING WITH REJECTION

Responsibility and duty are at the seat of every Goat's soul, so doing a good job that is accepted by others is of utmost importance for Capricorn writers. Rejection does not render them as emotional or paralyzed as it does other, more sensitive signs, but that doesn't mean Capricorns aren't affected on just as profound a level. One of the reasons why Capricorn writers are so careful about following the rules is that they will do anything to avoid rejection. However, when these writers receive an editorial dismissal, they soothe the hurt by diving right back into some sort of work-related project. While some signs flounder in the aftermath of rejection, Capricorns don their poker face and continue on, cool and collected, as if the setback didn't matter. It does matter, though, and in a big way, and Capricorns will begin a mission to prove they can overcome any adversity thrown in their path.

To better learn to deal with rejection, Capricorn writers need to take time to fully acknowledge the impact of rejection. Avoid stuffing your feelings down, and above all, learn to address issues head-on. When you ignore your feelings, they remain deep in your gut, where they fester and build until they manifest in a nasty eruption. You loathe failure, but if you plan to be a part of the writing industry, you must count on setbacks. There is nothing wrong with keeping your eyes on the prize, dear Capricorn. But remember that you should value the journey, not just arrival at your destination.

rejection DO's and DON'Ts

- **Do force yourself to venture from the tried and true.** Though you're all business and you prefer the established route, if you are receiving too many rejections, it may be time to get out of that rut and seek alternative paths to publication. You can't hope to bolster your credits if you refuse to look beyond your self-imposed borders.

- **Don't forget the human element.** Capricorns are notorious for their nose-to-the-grindstone approach to work. This is a praiseworthy approach in all business ventures, including those involving the publishing industry, but keep in mind that there is a human element involved in publishing as well. Anyone can write a technically perfect article, but that doesn't mean it's salable or what a publication wants. Decrease your chances of rejection by discovering the subtle human voice or point of view behind every publication, then target your work to fit in with that specific feeling. Readers of *Cosmopolitan* look for a different perspective and feel than do readers of *Jane*. Tap into your intuition and write from the heart as well as from your head.

- **Do allow yourself downtime.** Always striving for the next benchmark, Capricorns respond to rejection by pushing themselves even harder. Most people would find this a respectable trait; however, when you are too close to your work you often cannot see the solution right in front of your face. Take a few steps back at least once a week to gather up any rejections so you can look them over, take notes, and develop a new strategy. Pushing away from the desk on occasion is one of the smartest things you can do.

- **Don't go over the stated word limit.** Capricorns are usually by the book when it comes to following the rules, but on occasion they slip up and go past the suggested word count. They rationalize that there is so much information to pack into the article, a measly hundred words over the limit won't matter. Yes, it will. If your editor requests 1,000 words, don't turn in 1,150 instead. Cut those extra words until you're at or under the prescribed word count.

GIVING AND RECEIVING CRITICISM

Writers who expect critics to stroke their ego should probably bypass Capricorns. Those born under the sign of the Goat will give the news to them straight, whether their writing efforts are laudable or barely passable. Recipients of such criticism should be prepared to receive Capricorn assessments, good or bad, without any sugarcoating. Down-to-earth honesty is an essential part of the Goat's ethics, and that won't be compromised for anyone.

When Capricorns offer an opinion on a piece of writing, their aim is to let the author know what works and doesn't work for the reader so the writer can make the required changes. The goal is to try to help the author get closer to publication, not to hinder. *Why is it that others can't see that?* the Capricorn wonders. The answer lies in the manner of presentation. To the Goat, writing is a business and not a popularity contest. Their advice to aspiring writers is grounded and more than worthwhile. Writer signs who aren't as hardcore as Capricorns are should remember the method of delivery may not be so gentle. You'll receive unabashed honesty from Capricorns, but beware of the inadvertent sharp edges hidden in their critiques.

Capricorns don't relish receiving criticism. However, they will always consider comments and then separate the wheat from the chaff. When it comes to writing, Capricorns have the ability to detach themselves and listen to assessments of their work without prejudice. Afterward, they'll approach the comments they've received in a logical manner and decide which ones are relevant and should be incorporated into their work. No one enjoys criticism, but to Capricorns, if constructive advice is offered sincerely, they will take it into consideration.

10 PATHS TO PUBLICATION FOR CAPRICORN

1. Sell and repeat. As a Capricorn, you appreciate smart strategies that help you make more money. By retaining reprint rights on your articles, you'll open the door to repeat sales and additional income from articles that appear in more than one publication over time. Don't be afraid to negotiate rights in order to increase your chances of capitalizing on future sales.

2. Write what you know—at least in the beginning. If you majored in anthropology in college, where better to pitch to than an archaeology magazine? As a novice writer, in order to increase your chances of publication, you should focus on subjects in which you're knowledgeable. You may have to write on spec (on speculation, meaning you write the piece before the editor decides whether to purchase it) while you're making a name for yourself, but in the majority of cases, your efforts will pay off through larger and more frequent assignments.

3. Use a timeline. When Capricorn writers set a goal, they'll meet it come hell or high water. It's simply in their nature to press on until the deed is done—regardless of the obstacles. Gauging your progress can motivate and inspire you to increased productivity. Use index cards to chart your progress, and arrange them in a timeline on an office board. Jot down short- and long-term goals and target dates on the cards. Mark your progress at regular intervals (each week, two weeks, month, etc.).

4. Break with tradition. Tried-and-true freelance wisdom has it that each query must contain only one article idea. No longer so! Break out of archaic ways of thinking and pitch alternative ideas in the same letter. Though there is a subtle art to the multiple-idea query, this type of letter is a method of working smarter instead of harder. And while you prefer to stick to what's proven successful in the past, Capricorn writers must push forward to expand their options whenever the opportunity arises. Break out of the box and look for innovative ways to query.

5. Use templates. The various types of correspondence you'll be sending out as a working writer contain certain standard components. Cover letters and queries are two such correspondence types. By using a basic template letter in these cases, you can save time; instead of writing a new letter for every query or submission, pull up your template, make the necessary changes (to names, dates, addresses, etc.), and add in the specifics of the project. There is no need to start from scratch each and every time.

6. Cultivate ongoing relationships. There's nothing wrong with selling twenty articles to twenty different publications. However, instead of querying a new market for every article, try to develop steady relationships with certain editors. Once you've shown an editor you're a reliable and noteworthy freelancer, ask her if she would be willing to move you into a stable of trusted freelancers who are tapped for assignments on a regular basis.

7. Take notes. If you're new to the writing game, track down seminars and workshops designed to teach the basics of writing. Attend events with well-known headliners, and take every opportunity to connect with published authors presenting at conferences across the country. Listen intently, ask questions, and take copious notes. One surefire way to increase your chances of success is to get advice from a pro and incorporate those suggestions into your own work.

8. Write what you read. If you prefer fiction to nonfiction and you're looking to get published, the obvious advice is to write what you read. What's your favorite genre? Raving over romance? Hot over horror? Wild about westerns? Familiarity with a certain genre increases your chances of publication in that genre because you understand the pacing, rhythm, voice, and nuances of that genre. Pull out several of the books you've enjoyed the most as a reader, go through them one by one, and jot down what the authors did and did not do successfully in each book. Use those notes as guidelines when you sit down to pen your first book.

9. Keep it fresh. It's been said that there are a limited number of plots in the world of books. While that may be true—and there are reasons why certain plots sell consistently—your success in delivering a basic story plot has to do with your style and creativity as a writer. Yes, there's probably nothing new under the sun. For instance, secret-baby plots abound in the romance genre. However, not all secret-baby novels are written the same way. There's room for all sorts of unique combinations in scene, setting, and characterization. Increase your book's chances of publication by showing the editor a fresh view.

10. Give 'em the business. With your serious attitude and by-the-book approach to work, you're the perfect candidate for corporate freelancing. Develop a professional portfolio of your work—featuring sample brochures, letters, and reports—and approach various corporations in your city and beyond. Emphasize the cost-effectiveness of outsourcing their business writing, and if you're amenable to the idea, offer to do a pro bono piece to show them your stuff.

exercises for capricorn

Those born under the sign of the Goat conduct their lives in a no-nonsense and reliable way. Schedules and plans make them feel comfortable and safe. They are born for business and bred for leadership, easily shouldering the mantles of responsibility and accountability. Capricorns have the ability to write about any subject under the sun. They approach assignments on punk rock just as they would assignments on venture capitalists—they get the job done, no matter what it takes. In the course of doing their jobs, they can get mired in a repetitive mindset. The following exercises will assist Capricorn writers in applying their strengths and exploring new abilities.

1. Try something completely new every week. Pick one day from your writing week and discard all preset goals or schedules for that day. Each week, on your unplanned writing day, vow to engage in one or more activities you have never done before. Ever gone to a movie alone? If not, why not? Take yourself out of your safety zone and engage your senses in at least one activity that is new or different to you. Invite yourself (and no one else) to a movie, then pay attention to the atmosphere and the people around you. Make mental notes of behaviors—your own as well as others'. In order to write believable characters, you'll need to expose yourself to human nature in deeper ways. Learn to work without a safety net. You'll find that inspiration, by its very nature, appears not only when you least expect it, but when you haven't planned for it at all.

2. Outline your novel. Why is it you haven't begun that new novel, Capricorn? Employ your talent for planning by drafting a workable outline for each chapter of your soon-to-be-written book. That done, draft a schedule for each chapter's completion.

capricorn

FAMOUS CAPRICORN WRITERS

December 23, 1926	Robert Bly
December 25, 1924	Rod Serling
December 25, 1925	Carlos Castaneda
December 26, 1891	Henry Miller
December 26, 1956	David Sedaris
December 30, 1865	Rudyard Kipling
December 31, 1965	Nicholas Sparks
January 1, 1919	J.D. Salinger
January 3, 1892	J.R.R. Tolkien
January 6, 1878	Carl Sandburg
January 6, 1915	Alan Watts
January 9, 1908	Simone de Beauvoir
January 9, 1928	Judith Krantz
January 9, 1936	Anne Rivers Siddons
January 11, 1842	William James
January 13, 1832	Horatio Alger
January 19, 1809	Edgar Allan Poe

The ability of writers to imagine what is not the self, to familiarize the strange and mystify the familiar, is the test of their power.
—TONI MORRISON

Key personality traits: unconventional, visionary, inventive, detached

Symbol: the Water Bearer

Element: air

Ruling planet: Uranus

Qualities: positive, masculine, fixed

JANUARY 20– FEBRUARY 18

AQuarIus is the progressive, inventive sign of the zodiac. They are

free thinkers who are often so innovative and far ahead in their visions and ideas that the other writer signs—and the world at large—have a hard time keeping up with them. The phrase *he's from another planet* could be used to describe many an Aquarius, in fact. Described as otherworldly or eccentric, Aquarians begin to develop philosophical and spiritual bents at an early age. While they are often drawn to the sciences, many of them are just as fascinated by the psychic or supernatural realms. This doesn't mean they'll be fooled by charlatans or accept any harebrained theory put in front of them, however. Their minds are too logical and discerning for that. They are tolerant of others' views and will listen without prejudice, although they won't automatically swallow information others attempt to feed them. Science fiction and fantasy are excellent genres for Aquarius writers, but they're also attracted to history, biography, and the condition of mankind.

Water Bearers are also known as the humanitarians of the zodiac. They will fight for (and write about) causes they fervently believe in. Aquarians are intelligent, well read, and visionary. Because they often get lost in mental abstractions and ideas, they can come off as detached. They require freedom (both physical and mental) at all times, so the role of independent journalist or freelancer would appeal to them. Boredom is another word for death to the Aquarius, so editors who have a Water Bearer on their editorial staff would be wise to keep the assignments fresh and avant-garde. The quirkier the article or story, the more alluring it will be for the typical Aquarius scribe.

Four Foolproof Ways Aquarius Can Smash Writer's Block

1. Adopt a writing ritual. Certain tasks or objects signal your mind to prepare for writing. Find one or more writing rituals—grabbing a cup of coffee or turning on relaxing music—and incorporate them into your daily life. Each time you employ one of your rituals, it will serve as a mental anchor and help you slip into your creative mode with less effort.

2. Assume a new identity. If you're tired of wasting away in front of a blank page, maybe it's time someone else took over the job. Adopting the point of view of somebody else—whether that person is fictional or real—can help you write. Aquarians are imaginative by nature, so role-playing at the computer or in your journal should prove appealing. If you're adventurous, select a new writing identity for every other day of the week, and strive to write in that author's style—even if only for a short while—on that day. For instance, Mondays might be for Poe, Wednesdays for Coleridge, and Fridays for Dickinson.

3. Interview yourself. It's a rare Aquarius who doesn't have something to say; unfortunately, sometimes it's not so easy to get to that root idea. When you find yourself stuck in writing limbo and you're not sure where to go, interview yourself. What's on your mind today? Has your morning been routine, or did something out of the ordinary take place? Who are you today, as opposed to a year or five years ago? Make a list of your likes and dislikes. Expand that list and isolate at least three subjects for a brainstorming session.

4. Dump the baggage. On occasion, writer's block isn't about a lack of ideas—it's about emotions and life situations getting in the way. Aquarians are known for their enigmatic ability to come off as friendly and sociable while maintaining an air of cool detachment. Nonetheless, stress impacts you just as much as it does the next person. Are there any worries, fears, or concerns blocking your creative process? What are they? Give them voice for no more than five minutes, then shove them out of the way before you write.

DEALING WITH REJECTION

For the Aquarius writer, rejection isn't the most pleasant of experiences, but it's not the end of the world either. Nobody rejoices in being told no, but the Water Bearer listens to and learns from every rejection slip, then uses it as a springboard toward further improvement. Aquarians are quick studies, and it won't take long for them to turn disappointments into acceptances. These writers can be stubborn and high-minded at times, but they won't balk at taking the necessary steps to improve their work. However, if editorial suggestions aren't in accord with an Aquarian writer's personal code of honor, or if they cheapen the creative process, the Water Bearer will refuse to budge on his basic values.

Aquarians are much like Sagittarius, another optimist. The only difference is that you wouldn't be caught dead in those silly rose-colored glasses many Archers wear. No, your eyes are wide open and you are able to survey the publishing landscape in quick fashion. If one avenue of publication is blocked, it won't take long for the Water Bearer to find an alternative route. Aquarians have no shortage of ideas, and when one idea gets shot down, you won't hesitate to volley another into space. When an editor passes on your work, the blow will bring private discomfort, but you'll pick yourself up and dust yourself off in preparation for the next round.

Rejection Do's and Don'ts

- **Do be realistic.** In a perfect world, you would prefer to write for prestigious publications, but beginning writers usually aren't afforded that luxury. Being overly ambitious in your choice of targets may set you up for a flurry of rejections. It's true that you're often thinking on a higher level than most people, but until you gain expertise and a respectable number of clips, set your sights a bit lower and move upward at a steady pace.

- **Don't veer from the party line.** You think on a different level than most human beings, Water Bearer. And while you pride yourself on being unconventional, the rest of the world may be light years behind you. Resist the urge to detour from publication guidelines. You might have an innovative article idea, but no matter how brilliant the idea is, you won't sell it if it doesn't fit into the general scheme of what a magazine or publisher is looking for.

- **Do challenge yourself.** How many rejections did you garner last month? Set a goal this month to reduce that amount by one. Then push yourself to beat this goal each month. Instead of concentrating only on the number of queries or book proposals you're sending, focus also on reducing your rejections. Treat yourself each time you reduce your rejection rate by one per month while sending out the same number of submissions.

- **Don't go it alone.** Aquarians are often called the lone wolves of the zodiac because they retain at least a scintilla of aloofness even when they're in a crowd. As much as they give to others, they still reserve a sliver of privacy for themselves. Handling rejection alone isn't fun, and you don't earn points for keeping a stiff upper lip. Have regular get-togethers with a handful of writing buddies to hash over your collective hits and misses. Pass around your rejection letters and seek input from others.

GIVING AND RECEIVING CRITICISM

Aquarius writers are generous in helping other writers. They are able to balance a caring attitude with objective comments, and this makes you one of the most valued critique partners. Water Bearers genuinely care about improving the critiquee's writing. Aquarians will volunteer to assist in the revision process, but they won't push themselves on anybody. Altruistic by design, these writers believe it's their mission to lend a hand whenever there is a need. If you're stuck in the middle of a story and aren't sure where to go, call an Aquarius!

Scribes born under the sign of the Water Bearer are open and tolerant. They are always ready to accept different points of view and welcome varying opinions about their work. It is rare for Aquarians to lose their cool over a critique. Be as open and elaborate in your comments with them as you'd like. In fact, Aquarius writers cannot stand superficial responses to their writing. They will insist you view their work with nothing less than a discriminating eye. Afterward, they will ask questions and prod you for the deeper meaning of your appraisal. Come prepared with copious notes and solid reasoning, because they'll want to follow up with pointed questions.

10 PATHS TO PUBLICATION FOR AQUARIUS

1. Keep your writer's bookshelf well stocked. Aquarius writers love to read, so they welcome any excuse to purchase more books. Just as you should read in the genre you wish to write in, you should also build and update your personal library with writer's reference books. Make sure all bases are covered, from the basics of grammar and punctuation to plotting the perfect novel.

2. Know your audience. Many writers get so wrapped up in the writing process that they sometimes forget they aren't writing just for themselves, but also for an audience. This audience includes readers, editors, and agents, among others. If you have your eye on writing for publication and not solely for yourself, never lose sight of your audience. Before you put pen to paper, know the demographics of your average reader—age, occupation, hobbies, and education level, for starters.

3. Erase purple prose. Lyrical, imaginative writing can be a wonderful thing, but an overabundance of flowery, fifty-dollar words and self-indulgent run-on sentences will earn you a rejection in the blink of an eye. If you can make your point using ten words instead of fifty, please do. You may have an expansive vocabulary, but that doesn't mean you have to exhaust your entire list of words whenever you write.

4. Minimize adjectives and adverbs. Powerful writing relies on strong verbs and nouns rather than on weak adverbs and adjectives. Mark Twain once remarked, "If you see an adverb, kill it!" Twain was right. More often than not, adjectives and adverbs weaken a sentence's nouns and verbs.

5. Avoid wimpy writing. Would you rather have your character barge through a door or walk through it? Chances are you'd rather have your hero make a grand entrance than slink in like a whipped puppy. If you intend to make a positive impression on editors, favor lively writing featuring vibrant actions rather than lukewarm reactions. The page is a blank canvas; why drown it in muted tones when you can paint it with stunning swaths of color?

6. Get on with it! The days of rambling narratives are long gone. Setting and atmosphere are both important, but you shouldn't focus on these at the expense of the story or the characters. Writers who keep their audience on edge and get to the meat of the story win bonus points with readers and editors alike.

7. Engage in grassroots writing. Humanitarian and environmental causes strike a chord with Aquarius writers. Whether writing about vegetarianism, global warming, or another serious issue, you yearn to make a difference with your words. Approach activist organizations and find out if they are open to articles or columns written by freelancers. Have a sample of your work on hand just in case they request one. In addition, research book publishers that concentrate on eco-friendly subjects and study their backlist. Have a book idea they haven't covered yet? Pitch them a proposal or two!

8. Indulge in your thirst for logic. Science and technology are attractive subjects for Aquarius writers because Water Bearers possess such clear and logical minds. Seek out consumer publications geared to the reader who shares your interests, then query those markets.

9. Explore the avant-garde. While Scorpio writers are drawn to the bizarre, Aquarius writers are mesmerized by anything surreal or transcendent. Emergent philosophical schools and divergent cultural behaviors fascinate you. Get your foot in the door, then make an impression with alternative newspapers or underground weeklies.

10. Get radical. To call Aquarius writers progressive would be an understatement. You are the rebels of the zodiac, intent on shaking things up whenever the opportunity arises. Stirring the pot is one of your favorite pastimes. Whether you're on the front line of a social justice march or planted firmly on the ground at a sit-in, you are outspoken and unapologetic about your beliefs. A position as an on-scene correspondent or freelance journalist would prove a nice fit for you and your talents.

Exercises For Aquarius

As the nonconformists of the zodiac, Aquarius writers are touted as geniuses or visionaries. As writers, their strength lies in their ability to tap into the universal consciousness of humankind and translate the abstract to the concrete. Water Bearers straddle the logical and spiritual sides of life. They are as comfortable writing about hard physical sciences as they are writing about ethereal realms. They play the roles of practical scribe and dreamy poet by turns. These exercises are designed to home in on the aspects that make Aquarius an uncommon type of writer.

1. Personify freedom and independence. The ideals of freedom and independence ring true for you more than they do for any other writer sign, even Sagittarius. You dislike being pent up, fenced in, or restricted in any way. How would you personify freedom or independence, using concrete rather than abstract representations? What would freedom look like if it were a poem? How could independence be characterized in a story? Explore both of these possibilities.

2. Seek authenticity. Authenticity is an important goal in any Aquarius writer's life. The Water Bearer believes in living for a purpose and striving for honesty—even if the results aren't pretty. Ask yourself if you're living the writing life in the most authentic way possible. If you are, list the obstacles and setbacks you've encountered during the process of self-realization. If you aren't engaged in the writing life as authentically as you'd like, ask what is holding you back and why. Give your muse a voice, and let her have her say without censoring the thoughts or feelings that bubble out onto the page. Use the results of this exercise to refocus your intentions.

FAMOUS AQUARIUS WRITERS

January 22, 1561	Francis Bacon
January 25, 1759	Robert Burns
January 25, 1874	W. Somerset Maugham
January 25, 1882	Virginia Woolf
January 27, 1832	Lewis Carroll
January 28, 1873	Colette
January 28, 1933	Susan Sontag
January 29, 1860	Anton Chekhov
January 31, 1923	Norman Mailer
February 2, 1882	James Joyce
February 3, 1874	Gertrude Stein
February 7, 1885	Sinclair Lewis
February 7, 1812	Charles Dickens
February 8, 1955	John Grisham
February 8, 1928	Jules Verne
February 9, 1944	Alice Walker
February 12, 1938	Judy Blume
February 14, 1944	Carl Bernstein
February 17, 1912	Andre Norton
February 18, 1931	Toni Morrison

All God does is watch us and kill us when we get boring. We must never, ever be boring.

—CHUCK PALAHNIUK

Key personality traits: dreamy, empathic, compassionate, patient

Symbol: the Fish

Element: water

Ruling planet: Neptune

Qualities: negative, feminine, mutable

FEBRUARY 19–
MARCH 20

PISCES

PISCES are known as the sensitive, imaginative dreamers of the zodiac. Often it's said that those born under the sign of the Fish are living in their own dream worlds. To some extent, that might be true. Writers born under the sign of Pisces are natural understudies of human nature. They are empathic at the core and adept at understanding and interpreting the internal motivations of other human beings. Therefore, one of their biggest strengths is the ability to craft realistic, believable characters. Pisces writers are especially affected by those who are down on their luck, and they are masters at penning human-interest stories or spinning tales of a character triumphing over unfortunate circumstances. They are genuine in their concern for other people. This is what makes them such naturals for communicating with others through the written word.

On the other end of the spectrum, Pisces writers can be so introspective, shy, and sensitive that they have to guard against pessimism. Writing takes discipline and a tough hide, and these are things Pisces writers may have to consciously work on. Fish writers have a creative bent, and work as an artist or a writer is right up their alley. However, Pisces is not known as the most practical sign of the zodiac. Success in writing depends on attention to both the creative and business sides of the publishing industry. So, while Pisces will feel at home in any artistic endeavor, they'll need to brush up on business skills. Pisces may not like selling others on their work or on themselves as writers, but if they plan to succeed in publishing, they must consider it a necessary evil.

FOUR FOOLPROOF WAYS PISCES CAN SMASH WRITER'S BLOCK

1. **Control your emotions.** Your emotions underscore every ounce of your personality—whether you want to admit it or not.

Although today might bring nothing but a blank page or hours of staring at the computer screen, that doesn't mean tomorrow will be the same. Don't allow yourself to feed into self-destructive emotional patterns—they can worsen and prolong writer's block. Keep obsessive, unproductive thoughts under strict control. Remind yourself that tomorrow, if there's nothing else to write about, you can at least explore the previous day's stall through a personal essay. Once you start recounting, chances are you'll slip back into regular writing mode.

2. Take planned mental vacations. Planned distractions may give your mind a break and rekindle your creative spark. Reenergize your muse with a visit to the local cinema, fine art display, or concert in the park. Take in the sights and sounds, allowing yourself to melt into the moment. You'll return home rejuvenated and prepared to tackle your work with fresh eyes. Exposing all your senses to outside stimuli can boost your brain power and flood your mind with new ideas.

3. Use others as inspiration. As long as there are people in this world, there will be an overabundance of topics to write about. Most Pisces writers gravitate toward subjects that deal with the state of the human condition. Unlike Aquarius, who views problems of the human race on a global scale, you prefer to focus on the stories of individual lives affected by fortune, serendipity, or tragedy. Play on your strengths as an introspective, empathic soul, and you will be able to mine an endless array of possible articles and stories.

4. Dream on. The world of dreams is irresistible for most Pisces. Tap into your ability to enter the realm of fantasy by working on guided dreaming. Before bed, concentrate on your intent to enter into at least one dream during the night and to allow a subject, character, or story to be revealed to you, either whole or in part. Lull yourself to sleep by controlling your breathing and relaxing every part of your body, section by section. Then, behind closed eyes, focus your mind on a dark void—like a movie screen in your mind—and allow images to wash across your mental screen. Be sure you have a pen and paper or a voice-activated recorder at the ready so that, when you wake up, you can record the stories or characters you were introduced to in your guided dream exercise.

DEALING WITH REJECTION

Because Pisces writers so thoroughly enjoy their craft, it is important for them to receive regular reassurance that they're doing well. When an editor passes on an article, Pisces will take the rejection to heart in a big way. Those born under the sign of the Fish need to learn the art of detachment—not an easy task for one of the most sensitive scribes of the zodiac. Writing is a core component of the Pisces heart and soul, so the Fish must learn there is no personal slight intended when queries are returned with a form rejection attached. Just as a shopper peruses clothing items in a store, looking for the correct shape, color, or fit, editors and agents search for the right fit for their houses and agencies. Pisces must train themselves to consider their work as beautiful and inspirational overall, but not a perfect fit with every publication.

Pisces writers can soften the sting of rejection by putting their emotions into perspective. It's okay to feel disappointed when your latest masterpiece has been turned down, but it's quite another thing to let yourself dwell on the event. Keep a running list of all your successes and accomplishments, and refer to it on a regular basis. Also, realize your writing's worth is not determined solely by other people, but by yourself as well. The act of putting words on paper and baring your innermost thoughts to perfect strangers is a bold one, and should be applauded. Use your talent for introspection when rejections land in your mailbox. Comfort yourself with the advice you would give to any other writer in the aftermath of rejection.

REJECTION DO'S AND DON'TS

- **Do keep your emotions in check.** As a Pisces, you have a tendency to be sensitive and to take things too personally. Remember that rejection isn't designed to wound you. Constructive criticism and rejection are designed to help you hone your work and become a better writer. Detach yourself and realize you are marketing a product—your writing—and editors and publishers are not out to get you when they decide to pass on your work.

- **Don't obsess over what you did or did not do correctly this time around in your queries or submissions.** Mistakes do happen, but don't dwell on them. Instead of zeroing in on the negatives, make an effort to pick out all the things you did right. Determine what you need to change about your work or approach by studying the rejection letter for hints on how to improve. Then rework your piece, find new markets ripe for the picking, and give your precious writing wings to fly again.

- **Do kick your innate sense of patience into high gear.** If queries and submissions take patience, dealing with rejections requires even more of the same. Unless you are luckier than the average writer, you will suffer your fair share of rejection. Delve into that famous Piscean reserve of patience and resist the urge to give up on writing. Who are you fooling? You're a Pisces—you *have* to write! Buckle down, keep a level head, and answer each rejection by putting yet another article or query in the mail by the next day at the latest.

· **Don't ever call an editor about a rejection letter.** While you may want to plead your case and explain why you think your article fits the publication's needs, unless you are asked—specifically—to call an editor's office, avoid making that call. Editors are busy and often overworked; you won't endear yourself to them by calling to explain why they should give your piece another look. Accept the rejection and move to the next market.

GIVING AND RECEIVING CRITICISM

Give your work to a Pisces and you're in good hands. They are compassionate toward others and want to help in any way possible, although they are prone to holding comments back on occasion because they don't want to hurt anyone's feelings. Pisces writers are keenly aware that the sting of criticism can yield not-so-pleasant results. Never out to wound other writers, Pisces will present you with a nice balance of praise and constructive criticism. Because they work on an intuitive level, their comments will contain a degree of insight far beyond that of the normal writing assessment. Pisces writers look for the layers beneath the words and sentences. What's more, they care how you respond to their suggestions and will follow up with more explanation or discussion if you wish.

On the other hand, Pisces writers are gun-shy when it comes to criticism of their own work. All advice should be delivered in a constructive, gentle manner so the message gets through without being lost in the inevitable emotional response. The best policy is to remain honest and forthcoming with those born under the symbol of the Fish; however, don't come off as too harsh or matter-of-fact. These are the dreamers of the zodiac. When they hand over their stories or articles, they are handing you a piece of their hearts. They trust you won't crush their dreams or dash their hopes, and you should keep in mind that it isn't beneficial to them—or you—to do either.

10 PATHS TO PUBLICATION FOR PISCES

1. Play the numbers game. The more submissions or queries you send out, the better your odds for acceptance. Odds aren't just for horse races or Super Bowl bets; submitting for publication is about volume—the more articles you have in circulation, the better your chances of hitting the intended target. Set a goal to mail a specific number of queries each week, then stick to your goal no matter what.

2. Work now, dream later. Many writers start out as starry-eyed souls who dream of getting an advance check or snagging an agent. As one of the most avid dreamers of the zodiac, Pisces, you are no exception. Dreams and wishes come in handy because you can use them to set goals. However, without action, you'll never make any of your dreams a reality.

3. Keep the faith. Writing is hard work, and don't let anyone tell you different. Diligence has its rewards, so keep your spirits up by posting positive quotes around your office or subscribing to a motivational quote list on the Internet. Many writers throw in the towel when the going gets rough, but usually it's not long after the darkest moment that a ray of sunshine peeks through the clouds. Maintain a buoyant attitude by seeking out positive friends and family members. Avoid toxic naysayers and armchair quarterbacks who insist you'll never sell anything.

4. Make the connection. While you're keeping the faith, boost your Pisces idealism by connecting with professional scribes who can act as critique and advice partners. Find a mentor who is a published author or seasoned freelancer and model your work behavior after that person. Pisces sometimes break routine when duties become monotonous, so take your cues from writers who demonstrate consistent productivity. Ask them for tricks and tips for staying on track, then adopt those behaviors in your writing life.

5. Share the wealth—of knowledge, that is! You love helping others and will hardly ever say no to a reasonable request. Your generous Pisces nature is perfect for assisting new writers as they attempt to find their footing. Volunteer your services at a local community center or online as a writing forum moderator. Novice writers are always searching for mentors, and those born under the symbol of the Fish are adept at teaching and guiding others toward their dreams. If writing is a cause near and dear to your heart, extend your talents even further by penning how-to articles geared toward writing magazines and online writers' resource sites.

6. Enter contests. If you're shy about showing others your writing, test the waters by entering writing contests. You'll need to be cautious and take special care to enter only legitimate contests. Many writers balk at contests, especially if an entry fee is required, while others have no problem paying a fee to enter a reputable competition. Research contests before you enter any of them. Ask other writers, post on writers' forums, and peruse boards that report scams. When you're satisfied the competition you've selected is legitimate, give it your best shot. If you're short on credits, entering contests may pump up your portfolio.

7. Know your rights. Pisces prefers the creative aspect of writing over the dull matters of business, but eventually you'll need to develop business savvy to ensure you're reaping the full benefits of your efforts. When you sell your writing, your contract will outline which rights you are agreeing to give the publisher. Publishing rights can range from one-time and second serial to all rights, and there are many shades in between. Research what these terms mean and be prepared to negotiate for the best deal possible. Some great starting points on the Web for research on publishing rights include sites such as The Publishing Law Center (www.publaw.com), National Writers Union (nwu.org), and The American Society of Journalists and Authors (www.asja.org/pubtips/wmfho1.php). Each situation is different, so don't get caught by surprise. Study the ins and outs of rights before that first contract arrives in your mailbox.

8. Find a cause. You're a compassionate person who loves to be of service. Nonprofit organizations may be your avenue to publication. Many nonprofits need content for their newsletters, Web sites, and other informational materials. Make a list of nonprofits in your area and offer your services to them. While you may not land a paid position right away (you may end up working as an intern), you'll gain experience and publishing credits. Listing this type of experience on your writer's résumé can lead to bigger and better assignments.

9. Build your vocabulary. One key to salable writing is an extensive knowledge of words and phrases. If you don't already own a dictionary and a thesaurus (and I'm betting you do, since most Pisces natives love everything about words), purchase both. If your reference books are getting worn around the edges, throw them out and update your writer's library. Make a pact with yourself to learn a new word every week, and begin using the words you learn in your work whenever possible. Change things up a bit to show your readers how versatile you are.

10. Tap into your subconscious. With Neptune as your ruling planet, you are more open to the mystical and psychic realms than are other writer signs. Capitalize on this otherworldly connection by researching markets that specialize in paranormal subjects, such a Fortean events, aliens, psychic phenomena, and ghost hunting.

PISCES

Exercises for Pisces

Touched by Neptune's otherworldly influence, Pisces writers are dreamy scribes who straddle both the mundane and the magical sides of life. Blessed with a fertile imagination, Pisces writers can usually come up with more than enough material to write for decades on end. Problem is, although you have a lot in your head, sometimes it's so abstract and scattered that you aren't sure how to get it out on paper so it reads as you envision it. Stimulate your Pisces imagination and get your ideas into concrete form.

1. **Travel into the past.** Take a trip through time using your imagination and your writing. Select a century or time period in history you are fond of, then put yourself into that time through your words. If you could be anyone from history, who would you be? Don't select a notable person, but rather a general person such as a knight, landowner, merchant, or a woman in the suffrage movement. Envision yourself as that person and consider what a typical day would be like in that time period. Don't research this; instead, let your mind wander (close your eyes if need be). Write a page or two recounting what your life would be like as this fictional person, striving to record every detail you can think of. What was your name? Where did you live? How does it feel to live in someone else's body, in another time, for a day?

2. **Bring someone back with you to the present.** Think of a famous writer or poet from the past. Now bring that writer or poet into the twenty-first century, with all its technological inventions. Consider how you think that historical scribe would react to the modern conveniences you have as a writer. For example, if William Shakespeare suddenly plopped into London in the twenty-first century, how would the Internet help or hinder his work? If Will designed a Web site for himself, what would he put on it and

how would he explain and describe himself? Armed with DSL in her isolated room, how prolific would Emily Dickinson have become? Kick your wit into gear and write a humorous account of the modern-day meanderings of a famous writer or poet.

FAMOUS PISCES WRITERS

February 19, 1952	Amy Tan
February 19, 1965	Laurell K. Hamilton
February 21, 1903	Anaïs Nin
February 21, 1907	W.H. Auden
February 21, 1962	Chuck Palahniuk
February 28, 1970	Daniel Handler (Lemony Snicket)
March 2, 1904	Dr. Seuss
March 2, 1931	Tom Wolfe
March 6, 1806	Elizabeth Barrett Browning
March 7, 1964	Bret Easton Ellis
March 8, 1841	Oliver Wendell Holmes
March 12, 1922	Jack Kerouac
March 12, 1953	Carl Hiaasen
March 16, 1952	Alice Hoffman
March 18, 1932	John Updike
March 19, 1933	Philip Roth

writers on the cusp

What is a cusper, you ask? People who are born near the date when one sun sign switches to the next are born on the cusp. This means they likely share some traits of both the sun sign they were born under and the next closest sun sign. For instance, if you were born on November 23, you are a Scorpio/Sagittarius cusper and will share characteristics of both sun signs to some degree, even though you're technically a Sagittarius. Depending on the additional aspects of your chart, Scorpio might overshadow the Sagittarian influence in various areas of your life. You might be gregarious and jovial in your social life (Sagittarius), yet exhibit a more intense and focused demeanor in your work endeavors (Scorpio).

Determining whether you are a cusp writer can be tricky business in some circumstances. Many astrologers use several days before and after the sun sign changeover as a general guideline for determining who qualifies as a cusper. Unfortunately, what qualifies you as a cusper for one astrologer (or system) may not qualify you with another. I was born on December 17, so some astrologers would say I'm a Sagittarius/Capricorn cusper. Others would argue the cusp influence doesn't begin until December 19. In addition, because the position of the stars on any given date changes slightly from year to year, other astrologers prefer to judge cuspers by looking at the location of the sun in the zodiac sign at the time of birth. In basic terms, each sign's range is roughly thirty degrees in a Western astrological chart. Some astrologers consider cuspers to be those born when the sun is within three to five degrees of the transition point from one sign to another.

For the purposes of this book, you can use the cusp chart located below to find out if you were born on a cusp. For a more in-depth determination of all the sign and planetary positions at your birth, visit any number of astrology sites on the Web to obtain a free natal (birth) chart, or better yet, consult a local astrologer for a personalized reading. If you discover you were born on a cusp, locate the sun sign profiles for both signs and read them. You'll likely discover some traits that seem familiar to you and others that seem foreign to your nature. This is normal. Consider yourself special—you probably exhibit an interesting duality, and there are certain advantages to being a cusper.

CUSP CHART

Aries/Taurus	April 14–April 23
Taurus/Gemini	May 15–May 26
Gemini/Cancer	June 15–June 26
Cancer/Leo	July 17–July 27
Leo/Virgo	August 18–August 27
Virgo/Libra	September 17–September 27
Libra/Scorpio	October 18–October 28
Scorpio/Sagittarius	November 17–November 27
Sagittarius/Capricorn	December 17–December 27
Capricorn/Aquarius	January 14–January 24
Aquarius/Pisces	February 13–February 23
Pisces/Aries	March 15–March 25

The Aries/Taurus Cusp Writer

If you are serious about making your mark in the writing and publishing field, no one and nothing will stop you. Blessed with the high-powered drive of Aries and tethered in practicality by the earthy influence of Taurus, you are a driven writer who is bullish on meeting—and exceeding—your goals. Unlike some with Taurus influences, who may have a hard time getting started, the fire of Aries propels you to the next level of any writing project. Like quicksilver at the starting line, you also know how to pace yourself through the task until you complete it, often going above and beyond the requirements. Ruled by Mars and Venus, Aries/Taurus cusp writers have unrivalled passion, amazing drive, and boundless creativity.

THE Taurus/Gemini cusp writer

When Mercury and Venus come together, it makes for an unpredictable and engaging writer. Taurus/Gemini cusp writers pair an appreciation of beauty and the finer things in life with a streak of contagious enthusiasm, and they love to talk and communicate on any subject under the sun. Once they've made up their minds to follow a course of action, they are stalwart in their resolve to complete the task. As writers, they will be interesting in a multitude of subjects. They will not be easily deterred when it comes to rejection, and will plod along with determination until they manage an acceptance. The influence of Mercury blesses you with multitasking skills—have three assignments you need to complete in a short time period? For you, juggling them (and finishing them on time) will prove a snap.

THE Gemini/Cancer cusp writer

Still waters run deep, and so it is with you. These air/water cusp writers are driven by Mercury and the moon. Consequently, they are buoyed by genuine emotion, which is supported by sharp intellect. The expressive side of Cancer melds with the logical side of Gemini, so you are attracted to stories and characters that take you into the core of human experience. Not only are you able to empathize, you can also pull away and examine things objectively—an ability not all writers possess. This astrological combination could make you an excellent candidate for penning family memoirs. You may need an emotional outlet, and writing offers that outlet. Putting words on paper is cathartic and allows you to purge in a safe and private way. If you do not have a journal, you should start one today.

THE Cancer/Leo cusp writer

On the outside, everyone probably thinks you have confidence to spare. On the inside, you may carry deep insecurities no one ever knows about. These insecurities may also extend to your writing, whether you care to admit it or not. Because you are adept at managing just about anything, especially your home life, markets that focus on family life, crafts, or woodworking may best showcase your writing skills. Magazines that focus on nostalgia or genealogy could also be an outlet for your innate love of history and heritage. If you prefer fiction writing, books with a historical basis might be your cup of tea. These are merely suggestions, however. In the end, regardless of what genre or type of writing you pursue, you will put forth every ounce of effort you can muster—and then some!

THE Leo/Virgo cusp writer

Bywords for this cusp sign are organization and precision. The sun and Mercury mix in this cusp to deliver a powerful punch of personality. The normally reserved Virgo influence is trumped by the Leo's outgoing nature. This combination yields some of the most meticulous and creative writers of the zodiac. Not only will you dream up ingenious plots to rival the best, you will go the extra mile to research factual minutiae in order to make your story as accurate as possible. You are conscientious about your appearance and you know how to put on a superstar face, so book signings and public appearances will be a snap for you. Regardless of the material you are assigned, you are so skilled at composition that you make even the dullest subject seem divine.

THe VIrGO/LIBra cusp wriTer

Duty and impartiality are the keywords for your cusp sign. With the communicative touch of Mercury and the service-driven aspect of Venus, you are selfless and compassionate at heart. Because of these tendencies, you will want to use your writing skills for more than a personal sense of satisfaction. You will seek to assist others in your quest to understand and improve the world at large. Given your concern for justice and fairness in the world, you may find your niche in legal or social action. Markets that deal with health, medicine, or business affairs are also key writing areas to consider.

THe LIBra/scorpio cusp wriTer

Sensuous and brimming with desire, you can't be outdone in the sizzle and sex appeal you bring to your writing. When Venus and Pluto mix and mingle, the result is a scribe who can take his readers to the next level of sensual experience. Romance and mystery would be favorable genres for you to pursue. Life—everything you see, hear, touch, taste, and feel—is an ongoing wonder for you. When you put pen to paper, you weave stories overflowing with words that show instead of tell. You also have a built-in B.S. detector, and you can tell if another person is attempting to pull the wool over your eyes. With Scorpio's psychic influence and

Libra's desire for impartiality, you are insightful in connecting with the editors, publishers, and agents who can help you progress in your career.

THE SCORPIO/SAGITTARIUS CUSP WRITER

Freedom-loving Jupiter and brooding Pluto might make strange bedfellows at first consideration, but writers born on this cusp get the best of both worlds. As a Scorpio/Sagittarius cusper, you know when it's time to turn on the intensity and when it's time to kick off your shoes and have fun. Straddling both of these signs gives you the insatiable curiosity of the Centaur paired with the determination and unmatched focus of the Scorpion. When you see something, you train your laser-sharp attention on it, and it will eventually be yours. Affable around others, when it comes time to work, you won't tolerate shabbiness or dereliction of duty on the part of your co-workers. A writer born on this cusp will prove a pleasurable friend and a formidable foe. Don't mistake the warm smile for weakness in this one. Beneath that gregarious exterior lies a volcano of literary drive and ambition.

THE SAGITTARIUS/CAPRICORN CUSP WRITER

Jupiter and Saturn come together under this cusp alignment to produce a writer who is fun loving, yet serious when circumstances call for it. You know how to have fun and are touched by an abiding curiosity that is hard to satisfy. Because you are intellectual, scholarly fields may interest you, and it wouldn't be surprising to find your work published in academic journals. Though gifted with a clever sense of humor, you are attracted to serious subjects such as religion and philosophy. With your keen business sense, you could also succeed in writing for financial and business markets. You are a conscientious, persistent, and unflagging writer any editor would be proud to have on staff.

The capricorn/aquarius cusp writer

These cuspers make their entrance under the influence of the interesting combination of serious Saturn and uncommon Uranus. Forward-thinking and progressive in your approach to life, you will usually be drawn to genres that dwell on the fantastic, the cutting edge, or both—such as science fiction and fantasy. You are open-minded and willing to tackle any subject, and the outré does not easily shock you. Your work ethic is enviable, and once you start a writing project, your concentration is unbreakable. If you choose to collaborate with another writer, be sure his work ethic matches yours, because the earthy Capricorn in you will not suffer fools, loafers, or procrastinators.

The aquarius/pisces cusp writer

Pair a born innovator (fueled by the planet Uranus) and a consummate dreamer (courtesy of mystical Neptune) and what will you get? A writer who pushes the boundaries of creativity to the limit, that's what. Living can sometimes be a mystical experience to you, and you find people fascinating. You are often drawn to humanitarian stories, and you search for the deeper meaning beneath the surface. Everything—and every person—in your life provides a chance to translate these situations into writing. Those you meet in life may very well end up as composite characters in your short stories or novels—the thing is, you may not consciously know you create characters this way. Teetering between empathy and objectivity, you are adept at practicing detached compassion with your fellow human beings.

the pisces/aries cusp writer

Some might call you a loose cannon of sorts due to your enthusiastic ambition, but the truth is that you are an achievement-oriented, cause-motivated writer worthy of the highest regard. With the born leadership of Aries and the intuition of Pisces, you have a knack for homing in on words that aren't said (and thoughts that aren't publicly shared) and you use that knowledge for maximum impact. You don't do boredom, so carefully select genres or venues to keep things interesting. To whet your thirst for change, get involved in the writing community (if you aren't already). Start a writing group, or volunteer to assist with creative workshops and writing conferences in your area.

USING SUN SIGNS TO BREATHE LIFE INTO YOUR CHARACTERS

Need a brash, outgoing, me-centered character to play the role of a Hollywood glamour-puss named Roxy? Make her a Leo! Prefer to sculpt a more introverted and refined character to take the stage as an obsessive-compulsive literature professor who inadvertently gets himself into a bind and has to pry himself out of it? Put in some extreme Virgo tendencies and watch him fight against his external circumstances as well as his internal conflicts. Maybe you're working on a passionate romance and you need a gorgeous, ripped hunk to sweep your heroine off her feet. A dark, handsome Scorpio who screams sex should do the trick! No matter what the story or the character calls for, the attributes of each sun sign can provide you with excellent jumping-off points for crafty, unique characterization.

Listed below are short descriptions of the pure sun sign archetypes and how they would look and act in everyday life, including what careers would best suit them. What's the primary motivation for your Libra? What's the glaring character flaw of the Cancer archetype? Each profile lists the keywords and central attributes you need to craft your celestial characters. Use these basic descriptions to mold and shape those who people your stories and novels. Mix, match, and brainstorm a bit. For instance, what would happen if you paired a dreamy Pisces heroine with a brash, fast-talking Aries hero? Based on their astrological natures, would the pairing lead to love—or disaster? What internal conflicts could arise from such a relationship?

Key physical correspondence. According to ancient astrology, each sun sign corresponds to a particular part of the body. However, this focus may be positive or negative for your character. For instance, Sagittarius is associated with the hips and thighs. When you bestow physical strengths or weaknesses on your characters, use the physical correspondence for each sign as a means to emphasize special talents or to subtract from their abilities. Sagittarians are known as the natural athletes of the zodiac. Perhaps your character is an Olympic athlete training to compete in track-and-field events. All seems well—until an unexpected event leaves your character nursing a hip injury that threatens his career. How would this affect your character psychologically? Would he have the mental strength to overcome the one setback that threatens to turn his life upside down? As the writer, only you know for sure. Use these key physical correspondences to assist you in making your character's personality—and the story surrounding him—more believable and intricate.

Preferred color. Specific colors resonate with certain sun sign types. How does color play a role in your story, you might ask? There is a psychology to color, and certain emotions or feelings are associated with each band of the color spectrum. For instance, when you think of anger, what color comes to mind? Chances are, you thought of red before any other color. What about death and destruction? Black would be your most likely choice. Think of the color yellow—how does it make you feel? Happy, joyful, sunshiny? Building your character goes beyond creating personality traits. You also need to focus on appearance and the mood you want to portray in your characters' clothing and personal possessions. Scorpios make perfect villains—they are dark, intense, and cunning. A sleek black car would do the trick to convey that message, along with wraparound sunglasses on an angular face with a sharply chiseled jaw. Get the picture? Think beyond the main character's physical and mental features to every aspect of the person's life—such as the color of car she drives, the interior design of her house or apartment, the layout of her office, and her preferred clothing style.

Professions. Jobs say a lot about a person, and your character's career is no different. Some sun sign types work better in certain fields than others—both in reality and in fiction. Need a reliable accountant? Consider a Capricorn or a Taurus. How about a daredevil or international man of mystery? Scorpio or Aries is your man. When you build a character, you expect him to look, act, and speak a certain way. You also expect your character to have a fitting job. If you know you want a chatty, lightning-quick salesperson, chances are you should make your character a Gemini. On the other hand, if you intentionally want to wreak mayhem and create foreboding in the workplace (for whatever reason), turn your Gemini character's life upside down by putting her in a hellish job with an idiotic boss and incompetent co-workers.

Best paired with. Your characters need family, friends, and acquaintances. How to find the most harmonious mix? Check this section for ideas on the recommended zodiacal pairings for your story people. This section focuses on combinations that usually result in those best paired as friends, lovers, and people who like each other. In real life, compatibility with others hinges on more than the sun sign; in fact, compatibility can't be evaluated without a complete astrological analysis and comparison of both people's charts. This type of relationship astrology is called synastry. However, for your purposes in creating fictional characters, using the general sun sign types will suffice. Once you develop a more in-depth familiarity with each zodiac archetype, you can go a step further and combine various aspects—such as how a Cancer-sun/Sagittarius-moon person would interact with a Capricorn-sun/Virgo-moon partner.

Astrological opposites. Ever heard of the phrase "opposites attract"? The same can be found in sun sign astrology. In this section, these are zodiac signs your character may be drawn to because there is a strong, visceral attraction—most of the time for good but occasionally for ill. Intense chemistry usually exists between astrological opposites and the result is an irresistible urge to bond with this person. The astrologically opposite sun sign may possess qualities your sun sign lacks, and putting both signs together can make an interesting whole. However, due to the intense pairing of these signs, regardless of general compatibility, there is also a chance that competitiveness and one-upmanship could arise if negative character qualities are to the extreme or go unchecked. If you need an intense coupling for plot purposes, this is the way to go.

Best adversaries/villains. Need to find the best adversary or villain for your characters? Use this section for ideas on the recommended adversarial pairings for your story. This section focuses on combinations that usually result in pairings that may lead to conflict. While sun signs, as stated before, are only a slice of the astrological personality pie, this is a good jumping-off point for which sun sign characters could be pitted against one another.

Primary motivation. What is it that drives a particular sign? Under the primary motivation section, you'll learn the key force that motivates your character. Once you discover what makes a certain sign tick, you can use that driving force as a starting point for building conflict between your central character and those who interact with her. For instance, if your character is driven by the need for comfort and security, what would it take to shake

BREATHE LIFE INTO YOUR CHARACTERS

up her world? Use this knowledge of zodiacal psychology to flesh out story arcs and to force your character to change, grow, and learn over the course of the story or novel. Every person—real or imagined—is driven by at least one primary force. Find that force at the heart of your character and manipulate the circumstances for maximum conflict.

Primary flaw. Everyone has at least one weakness or flaw that makes life a challenge. Your characters should be no different. In fact, if your characters have no flaws—well, you don't really have believable characters at all. Without believable characters, your novel or short story will be dull and lifeless. The sections on flaws and weaknesses will assist you in identifying the Achilles heel of each character's astrological type. Once you understand each sign's specific personality deficiency, you can use that bit of information to tailor the story conflict.

The Aries Character

Key physical correspondence: the head

Preferred color: red

Professions: Driven by an insatiable need to succeed (and as quickly as possible!) the typical Aries, if there is such a thing, is fueled by the fires of the aggressive planet of Mars. Keywords for this fire-element sign are action and physicality. Aries are always on the go and they are the quintessential movers and shakers of the zodiac. Picture the fast-talking, flashy-dressing watch salesman on the street and you have an idea of how overwhelming the Ram's energy can be. When deciding what career your Aries character should have, consider anything that centers on action, excitement, risk, and power. Professions to consider include firefighter, athlete, paramedic, trial lawyer, actor, stunt person, executive producer, car sales-person, showgirl, bodybuilder, promoter, venture capitalist, and international businessperson. In addition, if anyone fits the mold of the self-employed entrepreneur, Aries most certainly does. The entrepreneurial spirit flows unchecked through the Ram's veins. Competitive and prepared to do what it takes to win at all costs, the Aries character won't be subtle in anything she does. Stick the Ram in a monotonous, boring job and you're sure to court disaster. Negative aspects of the Aries worker include failure to respect authority, lack of fol-low-through, and recklessness.

Best paired with: Gemini, Leo, Sagittarius, and Aquarius

Astrological opposite: Libra

Best adversaries/villains: Pisces, Taurus, Scorpio, Virgo

Primary motivation: achievement

Primary flaw: arrogance

THE TaUrUS CHaracTer

Key physical correspondence: the throat

Preferred color: pink

Professions: Purposeful and steady like the Bull, the Taurus character toils relentlessly in pursuit of her goals. Bound by the element of earth, these celestial characters aren't flashy or surprising. In fact, they are better described as sedate and durable. Like their Capricorn and Virgo cousins, Taurus work-ers do best when they are placed in the bedrock professions of society, where they can serve others in some capacity. Ad-mirable as a group worker but not as unremarkable as some astrologers would have you believe. Taurus also has an affinity for plants and artistic pursuits, especially those involving music. Suitable careers for the Bull might include gardener, landscaper, investment banker, composer, musician, singer, actor, producer, decorator, romance author, and actuary. Always under the touch of Venus, the Taurus character is dutiful in every chore, yet aware of the beauty of her surroundings. She can find a way to make any bland work atmosphere more comfortable and aesthetically appealing. Negative traits could include stubbornness, irritability, and procrastination.

Best paired with: Capricorn, Cancer, Virgo, Pisces

Astrological opposite: Scorpio

Best adversaries/villains: Aries, Gemini, Libra, and Sagittarius

Primary motivation: comfort

Primary flaw: stubbornness

THe GeminI cHaracTer

Key physical correspondence: the arms

Preferred color: yellow

Professions: Ruled by Mercury, the planet of communication, Geminis are naturally associated with professions that make the best use of their verbal and writing abilities. Those born under the sign of the Twins are suited to careers in broadcasting, sales, promotion, and publishing. Professional options for your Gemini character include (but aren't limited to) marketing specialist, disc jockey, advertising executive, salesperson, auctioneer, creative director, actor, talk show host, newscaster, publicity manager, telemarketer, and writer.

Ready for action all the time and a bit restless unless they have a million things on the back burner, pure Gemini characters will be talkative, outgoing, and idealistic when it comes to their profession. The only possible drawback to employing your Gemini character would be lack of follow-through. This tendency is an outgrowth of boredom and stasis, however. Keep your dual-natured character busy and motivated and you'll have the perfect productive worker.

Best paired with: Aries, Leo, Libra, and Aquarius

Astrological opposite: Sagittarius

Best adversaries/villains: Cancer, Capricorn, Taurus, Scorpio

Primary motivation: communication

Primary flaw: restlessness

THe cancer cHaracter

Key physical correspondence: the chest

Preferred color: white

Professions: Driven by emotion and buoyed by intuition, moon-influenced Cancer characters delight in careers that allow them to be of service to others. Born nurturers, they gravitate toward any profession that offers them a chance to make life better for other people. Because they are a water sign, they may also be drawn to bodies of water of any size, from the Mississippi River to the Pacific Ocean. Attractive professions for your Cancer character may include doula, nurse, marine biologist, childcare worker, history teacher, genealogist, obstetrician, pediatrician, chef, geriatric caregiver, and riverboat captain. Cancers have a desire to be needed by others, so if you want your moon child to be happy, it's essential you place her in a position that allows for teaching and sharing in one way or another, either formally or informally. The Crab will perform duties in a thorough and complete manner and will generally get along with most co-workers, as long as they're given adequate space. On occasion, Cancer can get downright crabby (pardon the pun), so moodiness is a drawback of this sign. At the utter extreme of the negative personality scale, the Cancer worker may come off as an oversensitive hermit who reads more into other people's behavior than is really there and who pouts at the drop of a hat.

Best paired with: Taurus, Virgo, Scorpio, and Pisces

Astrological opposite: Capricorn

Best adversaries/villains: Aquarius, Gemini, Leo, Sagittarius

Primary motivation: security

Primary flaw: moodiness

The Leo Character

Key physical correspondence: the heart

Preferred color: gold or orange

Professions: Warm and bright as the sun this sign is ruled by, your Leo character is happiest when you keep her firmly in the spotlight. There is no shortage of Lions in Hollywood (check it out sometime—look for those with sun signs and ascendant signs in Leo), so it goes without saying that if your book requires a diva or an ambitious starlet, then this is the sign you should consider above all others. Other appropriate professions for your Leo character include dancer, hostess, professional organizer, hairstylist, actress, bestselling novelist, literary agent, politician, cosmetologist, and celebrity attorney. The Lion needs attention and praise, so if you must give her a less-than-regal profession, at least make sure she is ranked as the top employee at the company. Terrific organizers by nature, your Leo character makes hard work look like child's play. Leo's bossiness and tendency to patronize (not everyone can be as organized and efficient as Leo, can they?) can cause conflicts with co-workers. Your Leo worker may also come off as power hungry and overly domineering. The man-eating, high-powered female executive who chews people up and spits them out would be a prime example of the exaggerated negative Leo work archetype.

Best paired with: Aries, Gemini, Sagittarius, and Libra

Astrological opposite: Aquarius

Best adversaries/villains: Cancer, Capricorn, Pisces, Virgo

Primary motivation: recognition

Primary flaw: self-centeredness

THe VIrGO CHaracter

Key physical correspondence: the stomach

Preferred color: brown or peach

Professions: With their precise natures, your Virgo characters would make excellent accountants, engineers, scientists, mathematicians, psychiatrists, dieticians, nurses, mechanics, dental hygienists, secretaries, surgeons, veterinarians, librarians, editors, teachers, and financial planners, to name but a handful. Regardless of the profession you choose for your

Virgo, remember that this sign is connected with Mercury, the planet of communication. Like Geminis, Virgos are adept at communication, but they aren't as outgoing or assertive as Gemini natives. Virgo works on more of an internal level, and expresses more with action than talk. No matter what career a Virgo character undertakes, you can be sure she will perform her duties in a precise and accurate manner. Taken to the extreme, negative aspects of a Virgo worker could include analretentiveness and a tendency to nitpick and overanalyze.

Best paired with: Capricorn, Taurus, Cancer, Scorpio

Astrological opposite: Pisces

Best adversaries/villains: Aries, Aquarius, Leo, Libra

Primary motivation: accuracy

Primary flaw: criticism

The Libra Character

Key physical correspondence: the kidneys

Preferred color: blue

Professions: Libras are the diplomats of the zodiac. They are blessed with an ability to listen to all sides and be impartial in all matters. Sensitive and aware, characters born under the symbol of the scales are constant seekers of parity and decorum. Balance and peace are important to Libra characters, so careers that bring structure out of chaos appeal to this sign. Desirable professions might include model, artist, astrologer, diplomat, mediator, architect, judge, actor, poet, dancer, fashion designer, psychologist, and comedian. Like Aquarians and Geminis, Libras are ruled by the element of air, which corresponds to the intellect. They have a deep dislike of crass or ugly behavior, and they appreciate refined people and surroundings. Eager to please others, Libras work well in groups and strive to maintain the status quo whenever possible. They are able to see all sides of a situation, so while their input may be valuable, they should not be put in the position of having to make immediate decisions (the phrase *rush to judgment* is foreign to their mode of thinking). You would give grief to your Libra character by placing her in an atmosphere filled with chaos, enmity, and favoritism. Upset the equilibrium of a Libra character, and the result will be vacillation, codependency, and reluctance.

Best paired with: Gemini, Leo, Sagittarius, Aquarius

Astrological opposite: Aries

Best adversaries/villains: Taurus, Scorpio, Pisces, Virgo

Primary motivation: balance

Primary flaw: indecisiveness

THe scorpio character

Key physical correspondence: the genitalia

Preferred color: black

Professions: If you need a sultry or dangerous character—perhaps an assassin or a con artist—then Scorpio is the right sign for you. Always intense and deadly accurate no matter what task she undertakes, your Scorpio character will excel in a number of interesting professions, including sex therapist, detective, escort, international spy, psychic, military commander, religious leader, actress, magician, king/queen/president, CEO, and scientist. As you select the perfect career for your Scorpio character, remember that this sign is connected with Pluto, the planet of mystery and hidden meanings. Like their water-element cousins, Cancer and Pisces, Scorpios harbor complex emotions. However, unlike the other two signs, Scorpios prefer to keep their darkest secrets and hurts under wraps so no one can expose their weaknesses. Perhaps this is one reason why those born under this sign make such excellent actors—they are adept at wearing masks and practicing sleight of hand. They are cautious and thorough, and they do not suffer fools gladly. With their sixth sense and uncanny ability to nail others' hidden intentions, Scorpios are naturals for solving crimes or unearthing complex mysteries. On the shadow side of the Scorpion are such unsavory traits as jealousy, possessiveness, and cruelty.

Best paired with: Capricorn, Cancer, Virgo, Pisces

Astrological opposite: Taurus

Best adversaries/villains: Aries, Gemini, Libra, Sagittarius

Primary motivation: desire

Primary flaw: possessiveness

THe saGITTarIus CHaracTer

Key physical correspondence: the hips and thighs

Preferred color: purple or indigo

Professions: Sagittarius characters are happiest when you place them in careers that allow plenty of independence, freedom, and intellectual challenge. Archers are curious, they love to explore, and they are entranced by religion, philosophy, and law. A monotonous, repetitive job without mental or physical stimulation would be the kiss of death for their gallivanting and inquisitive souls. Your Sagittarius character would feel right at home as a movie producer or director, judge, preacher, archaeologist, travel agent, cruise ship or tour director, explorer, professor, journalist, stage performer, flight attendant, or human resource manager. Jupiter, the ruler of the Archer, is expansive and demands freedom of thought and expression. The downside of this freedom is that many Sagittarians blurt out exactly what they're thinking without censoring any of it. They don't mean to pierce bystanders with their sharp arrows of truth and are often surprised when the recipients of their criticism react like a wounded puppy. Workers born under this sign are the most positive people employers could ever hope to hire. When everyone else is screaming that the sky is falling, the optimistic Sagittarius will find the silver lining in the lowering clouds. A negative Sagittarian worker would be argumentative, lazy, unreliable, and restless.

Best paired with: Aries, Leo, Libra, and Aquarius

Astrological opposite: Gemini

Best adversaries/villains: Cancer, Capricorn, Taurus, and Scorpio

Primary motivation: freedom

Primary flaw: bluntness

The Capricorn Character

Key physical correspondence: the knees, bones, and teeth

Preferred color: gray

Professions: Like the Mountain Goat that symbolizes this sign, the Capricorn character is as sturdy and unbreakable as the rocky summit she stands upon. Reliability is the lynchpin of the Goat's character, and although you won't find the daring or excitement of other signs in this personality, you will find a loyal and efficient employee. As an earth sign, Capricorn characters will always do best toiling away at salt-of-the-earth or foundational careers. Keep your Goat happy by giving him a job as an accountant, manager, quality control inspector, stockbroker, banker, government worker, politician, dentist, orthopedic surgeon, engineer, business owner, economist, teacher, or auditor. Influenced by Saturn, the Capricorn character is serious in both work and play. They are well grounded and are serious about anything that has to do with money: making it, investing it, and spending it (which they do wisely, of course). An unhappy Capricorn worker will exhibit distasteful tendencies such as stinginess, arrogance, detachment, and elitism.

Best paired with: Taurus, Virgo, Scorpio, Pisces

Astrological opposite: Cancer

Best adversaries/villains: Aquarius, Gemini, Leo, Sagittarius

Primary motivation: competence

Primary flaw: inflexibility

The Aquarius Character

Key physical correspondence: the calves and shins

Preferred color: aqua

Professions: Known as the innovators of the zodiac, Aquarians are always ahead of their time—so much so that bosses and coworkers might describe Water Bearers as unusual, odd, or eccentric. On the list of harmonious professions for the Water Bearer are activist, inventor, astrologer, astronaut, writer, director, lobbyist, politician, scientist, military strategist, pilot, and professor. Proud to be recognized as the smart rebels of the zodiac, these individuals are keenly aware of their abilities and often show others how to do the job better and in less time. As an air sign, Aquarius characters are intellectuals concerned with the state of humanity. They require freedom and independence in order to function at their best. As with their celestial cousins, Gemini and Libra, quick thinking is one of their gifts. Unlike the other signs, however, Aquarius pushes the boundaries of the mundane and isn't afraid to think outside the box—even if it makes her unpopular. Fairness and equality are buzzwords for all Aquarians, so it's important to put them in positions that allow them to champion causes that will improve the social condition on a grand scale. Want to get on the bad side of the Water Bearer? Try micromanaging them, and you'll see nasty results in the blink of an eye. The darker side of Aquarius is aloofness, elitism, and cynicism.

Best paired with: Aries, Gemini, Libra, Sagittarius

Astrological opposite: Leo

Best adversaries/villains: Cancer, Capricorn, Pisces, Virgo

Primary motivation: innovation

Primary flaw: eccentricity

THE PISCES CHARACTER

Key physical correspondence: the feet

Preferred color: sea green

Professions: Symbolized by two fish swimming in opposite directions, Pisces characters spend their lives with one foot in the mundane and the other foot in the magical. The premier dreamers of the zodiac, the Pisces worker is imaginative, inventive, and creative. Ruled by the element of water, these natives are sensitive and carry their hearts on their sleeves. Never give a Pisces character monotonous or boring work—they need unique ways to express themselves and their feelings. Perfect career matches for one born under the Fish would include actress, painter, astrologer, singer, counselor, yoga instructor, sculptor, writer, diver, anthropologist, inventor, and philanthropist. Neptune exerts a strong pull over Pisces personalities, so expect a certain otherworldly quality to these individuals. They are apt to come up with ideas for contraptions no one else has even thought of yet. If you're on the hunt for a quirky character for your novel—perhaps a gypsy fortuneteller or an offbeat performance artist—this sign might be the one that fits the bill. Looking to cause conflict in a work setting? Expose your Pisces to harsh criticism or draconian work conditions, and that should do the trick. Disgruntled workers react with emotional outbursts, irrational actions, and extended pouting sessions.

Best paired with: Taurus, Cancer, Virgo, Scorpio, Capricorn

Astrological opposite: Virgo

Best adversaries/villains: Aries, Aquarius, Leo, Libra

Primary motivation: idealism

Primary flaw: oversensitivity

Bev Walton-Porter is a Colorado-based professional writer who has published hundreds of columns, articles, and reviews since she began freelancing full-time in May 1997. She first began writing for publication in 1982.

Bev is a member of the Authors Guild and Pikes Peak Writers. In 2004, she collected several of her previously published articles in *The Complete Writer: A Guide to Tapping Your Full Potential*. She publishes Scribe & Quill, an award-winning newsletter for writers.

Bev began studying astrology thirty-two years ago, at the age of nine. By the time she was twelve, she had drawn up her first natal chart the old-fashioned way, using an ephemeris, a chart that shows the positions of the sun, moon, and planets on any particular day and time in a given year. She is an Associate Member of the American Federation of Astrologers (AFA).

When she is not writing, she is pursuing advanced studies in communications and philosophy at the University of Colorado at Colorado Springs. Her favorite author is Stephen King. For more information, visit www.bevwaltonporter.com.